I0160344

Frost of Spring Green

A Collection of Poetry

Frost of Spring Green Poetry Series – Book 1

Karen Jean Matsko Hood

CURRENT AND FUTURE POETRY BOOKS
by Karen Jean Matsko Hood

Frost of Spring Green Poetry Series

Frost of Spring Green – Book 1
Chill of Summer Blue – Book 2
Bloom of Autumn Gold – Book 3
Warmth of Winter White – Book 4

Hood Poetry Series

Cupboard Door – Book 1
Feminine Muse – Book 2
Feminist Revival – Book 3
Haiku Dollops – Book 4
Hummingbird Hover – Book 5
In Honor of Adoption – Book 6
In Honor of Take Back the Night – Book 7
Poems in Shapes – Book 8
Segments – Book 9

Regional Poetry Books

Hood Regional Poetry Series

American Pride – Book 1
Cruzan Frangipani – Book 2
Glacier National Park – Book 3
Iowa Cornsilk Rambles – Book 4
Montana Big Sky Blues – Book 5
Oregon Coast Tides – Book 6
Schweitzer Mountain Mist – Book 7
Washington Evergreen Thoughts – Book 8

Praise for Frost of Spring Green
A Collection of Poetry
Frost of Spring Green Poetry Series – Book 1

... "*Frost of Spring Green*, this delightful and insightful poetry book has proved to be a inspiration and is creatively witty with the use of heartfelt words and shape poems. It was a delight to read and I recommend this book to all who enjoy and read poetry books this is truly a book for all ages." ...

Mary Scripture-Smith
Graphic Designer

... "*Frost of Spring Green* evokes an awakening of the inner-self. Karen Hood's poetry is both eloquent and enlightening. Her words have the ability to transport readers to places of ponder, tranquility and inspiration. You don't have to be a scholar to appreciate the depth of character, atmosphere and emotion that emerges from these pages.

Instead of logging on or channel surfing tonight, feed your imagination with a little food for thought ... *Frost of Spring Green*." ...

Kimberly Carter
Spokane, WA

Praise for Frost of Spring Green
A Collection of Poetry
Frost of Spring Green Poetry Series – Book 1

... "Karen Hood's first collection of poetry, *Frost of Spring Green*, is a masterful collection of poems in a wide range of topics ...

Hood's poetry is clear and confident, elegant in its simplicity. She is adept at crafting layers of meaning and impact that work on the heart over time, providing powerful insight into the wonders of the natural world and the human condition.

Frost of Spring Green's imagery is powerfully visual, painting vivid pictures that are poignant and breathtaking whether the subject is a beautiful flower or mountain vista, or the cardboard box an orphaned, homeless child has used to construct a home for herself.

... a compelling read for anyone who enjoys poetry. " ...

Kim Saunders

... "Just as each of us has a favorite comfort food, this volume of poetry is comfort food for the human spirit. The poet relates simple memories in a way that the reader can vividly experience. She is both thoughtful and thought provoking. Her poetry is naturally relaxing and a powerful community action stimulant. I find myself going back again and again to this book." ...

Dr. James G. Hood
Editor

Spiritual Poetry Books

Hood Spiritual Poetry Book Series

Embers – Book 1
Memories Last – A Time to Grieve – Book 2

Reflection Series

Morning Reflections – Book 1
Evening Reflections – Book 2
Reflections for Women – Book 3

Hood Children's Poetry Books Series

Under the Lilacs – Book 1
There's a Toad in the Hole…A Big Fat Toad in the Hole – Book 2
Stinky Feet and Other Unpleasant Items – Book 3
There's a Goat in the Boat – Book 4

Poetry Books for Young Adults and Teens (Ages 13-18)

Hood Young Adults and Teens Poetry Book Series

What's Up? – Book 1

Many of the above listed books are also available in bilingual and translated versions. Please contact Whispering Pine Press International, Inc., for details.
This list of books is not all-inclusive. For a complete list please visit our website or contact us at:

Whispering Pine Press International, Inc.
Your Northwest Book Publishing Company
P.O. Box 214, Spokane Valley, WA 99037-0214 USA
Phone: (509) 928-8700 | Fax: (509) 922-9949
Email: sales@whisperingpinepress.com

Publisher Websites:

Main Website: WhisperingPinePress.com
Online Store: WhisperingPinePressBookstore.com
WordPress Blogs: WhisperingPinePressBlog.com
WhisperingPinePressKidsBooks.com
WhisperingPinePressTeenBooks.com
WhisperingPinePressPoetry.com

Karen Jean Matsko Hood

Author Website: KarenJeanMatskoHood.com
Online Store: KarenJeanMatskoHoodBookstore.com
Author Blog: KarenJeanMatskoHoodBlog.com
Kids Books: KarensKidsBooks.com
Teen Books: KarensTeenBooks.com

Author's Social Media

Like or Friend the Author on Facebook:
https://www.facebook.com/KarenJeanMatskoHoodAuthorFanPage

Follow the Author on Twitter:
https://twitter.com/KarenJeanHood

Google Plus Profile: http://google.com/+KarenJeanMatskoHood

Pinterest: https://www.pinterest.com/KarenJMHood/

LinkedIn: http://www.linkedin.com/in/KarenJeanMatskoHood

YouTube: http://www.youtube.com/KarenJeanMatskoHood

Instagram: http://instagram.com/KarenJeanMatskoHood

MySpace: https://myspace.com/KarenJeanMatskoHood

Frost of Spring Green

A Collection of Poetry

Frost of Spring Green Poetry Series – Book 1

Karen Jean Matsko Hood

Published by:

Whispering Pine Press International, Inc.
Your Northwest Book Publishing Company

P.O. Box 214
Spokane Valley, WA 99037-0214 USA
Phone: (509) 928-8700 | Fax: (509) 922-9949
Email: sales@whisperingpinepress.com
Websites: www.WhisperingPinePress.com
www.WhisperingPinePressBookstore.com
Blog: www.WhisperingPinePressBlog.com

SAN 253-200X
Printed in the U.S.A.

Published by Whispering Pine Press International, Inc.
P.O. Box 214
Spokane Valley, Washington 99037-0214 USA

For sales outside the United States, please contact the Whispering Pine Press International, Inc., International Sales Department.

Book and Cover Design by Artistic Design Service
P.O. Box 1782
Spokane Valley, WA 99037-1782 USA
www.ArtisticDesignService.com

Library of Congress Number (LCCN): 2014902280

Hood, Karen Jean Matsko
    Title: Frost of Spring Green: A Collection of Poetry
Frost of Spring Green Poetry Series – Book 1
    p.   cm.

ISBN: 978-1-930948-91-4   case bound
ISBN: 978-1-93094-892-1   perfect bound
ISBN: 978-1-59434-733-7   large print edition
ISBN: 978-1-59210-535-9   audio compact disc
ISBN: 978-1-930948-98-3   audio recording downloadable
ISBN: 978-1-59210-000-2   E-PDF
ISBN: 978-1-59210-948-7   E-PUB
ISBN: 978-1-59434-877-8   E-PRC
Soon to be available on Whispersync

First Edition: January 2014
1. Title (Frost of Spring Green: A Collection of Poetry
Frost of Spring Green Poetry Series – Book 1)

Dedications

To God, who makes all mornings possible.

To my husband and best friend, Jim.

To our seventeen children: Gabriel, Brianne Kristina and her husband Moulik Vinodkumar Kothari, Marissa Kimberly and her husband Kevin Matthew Franck, Janelle Karina and her husband Paul Joseph Turcotte, Mikayla Karlene, Kyler James, Kelsey Katrina, Corbin Joel, Caleb Jerome, Keisha Kalani Hiwot, Devontay Joshua, Kianna Karielle Selam, Rosy Kiara, Mercedes Katherine, Jasmine Khalia Wengel, Cheyenne Krystal, and Annalise Kaylee Marie.

To our grandchildren and foster grandchildren: Courtney, Lorenzo, and Leah.

To my brother, Stephen, and his wife, Karen.

To my husband's ten siblings: Gary, Colleen, John, Dan, Mary, Ray, Ann, Teresa, Barbara, Agnes, and their families.

In loving memory of my mom, who passed away in 2007; my dad, who passed away in 1976; and my sister, Sandy, who passed away due to multiple sclerosis in 1999.

To Sandy's three sons: Monte, Bradley, and Derek. To Monte's wife, Sarah, and their children: Liam, Alice, Charlie, and Samuel and their foster children. To Bradley's wife, Shawnda, and their children: Anton, Isaac, and Isabel.

To our foster children past and present: Krystal, Sara, Rebecca, Janice, Devontay Joshua, Mercedes Katherine, Zha'Nell, Makia, Onna, Cheyenne Krystal, Onna Marie, Nevaeh, and Zada, our future foster children, and all foster children everywhere.

To the Court Appointed Special Advocate (CASA) Volunteer Program in the judicial system which benefits abused and neglected children.

To the Literacy Campaign dedicated to promoting literacy throughout the world.

Frost of Spring Green

A Collection of Poetry
Frost of Spring Green Poetry Series – Book 1

Gift Inscription

To: _____

From:_____

Date: _____

Special Message: _____

_____

_____

_____

_____

_____

_____

_____

*It is always nice to receive a personal note to
create a special memory.*

www.WhisperingPinePress.com
www.WhisperingPinePressBookstore.com

Professional Acknowledgements

A grateful acknowledgement is made to the following magazines and publications where certain poems have appeared in various forms:

Poetry Publications	Title of Poem(s) Published
Abiko Annual	*Cradle, Curved Path, Lavender Visitors, Oaken Planks*
Abraxis Publications	*Oaken Planks, Moonlit Sun*
Aguilar Expression	*Hauser Lake*
Black Spring Review	*Embers*
Blind Man's Rainbow	*Burnt Stones, Embers, Cupboard Door, Latent Knowledge, Trout Fishing*
The Blind Press	*Latent Knowledge, Burnt Stones*
Chaff	*Curved Path*
Challenger International	*Trout Fishing*
Children Far and Wide	Various Poems
Children's Churches & Daddies	*Apple Crates, Cupboard Door*
Conservatory of American Letters	*Cattleya Blossom, Fresh Air, Hooves Pounding*
Cosmic Trend	*Lavender Visitors*
Dream International Quarterly	*Cupboard Door, Trout Fishing*
DGR Publications	*Breath of View*
Experimental Poet	*Cupboard Door*
Fauquier Poetry Journal	*Cupboard Door*
Flame	*Norse Viking*
Free XpresSion Magazine	*Cradle, Cupboard Door, Gray Spring, Indian Paintbrush*
Gaited Horse International Magazine	Various Poems
Gentle Reader	*Carpenter's Daughter, Moonlit Sun, Oaken Planks*
GSPR	*Norse Viking*

Haight Ashbury Literary Journal	*Cupboard Door*
Hawaii Pacific Review	*Cupboard Door*
Icelandic Horse and Travel Magazine	*The Icelandic Horse*
Konfluence	*Cupboard Door*
Lone Stars Magazine	*Cupboard Door, Indian Paintbrush, Lavender Visitors, Reunion, Tamarack, Casket, Christmas Cactus, Storm Cloud, The Dove and the Eel, Ever Wonder Why, Meadow Memories, Closet Conundrum, Laborers, Autumn*
Louisville Review	*Indian Paintbrush, Lavender Visitors*
Lucid Moon	*Ant Hill, Nutcracker, Treehouse, Roller Coaster, Radio Noise*
Magnolia Quarterly, Gulf Coast Writer's Assoc.	*Carpenter's Daughter, Cradle, Cupboard Door, Curved Path*
Marginalia Magazine	*Apple Crates*
Matchbook	*Apple Crates*
Midnight Star Publications	*Indian Paintbrush*
Munna Takeena	*Carpenter's Daughter, Cradle, Curved Path*
New Mirage Quarterly	*Dance*
Nomad's Choir	*Indian Paintbrush, Spilled Wine and Steel Drums*
Northern Stars Magazine	*Carpenter's Daughter, Gray Spring, Indian Paintbrush, Barefoot Girl, Mystery Bundle, Grandpa's Cradle*
Old Red Kimono	*Silver Reunion*
Pacific Review	*Frost of Spring Green*
Poetic License	*Apple Crates, Gray Spring, Lemons, Moonlit Sun, Profane Verse*
Poetry.com	*Pollen Beyond My Reach, Autumn Snow*
Prairie Winds	*Cupboard Door*
Provincetown Magazine	*Below the Hawk He Walks, Breath of View*
The Poet Band Company	*Bubble Bath*
The Poetry Explosion Newsletter	*Carpenter's Daughter*

Quantum Leap	*Trout Fishing*
Ralph's Review	*Moonlit Sun, Trout Fishing*
RB's Poets' Viewpoint	*Meadow Music*
Rivers Edge	*Sleepless, Candle Flicker, Theories and Equations, Conception, Driving Through Missoula, Morning, Daylilies, Life*
Romantic Outsider	*Meaningful Eyes*
Scroll	*Cradle, Curved Path, Apple Crates, Gray Spring, Trout Fishing*
Small Brushes	*Pike Street Market*
Soul Fountain	*Oaken Planks, Pollen Beyond My Reach, Reunion*
Splizz	*Casket, Bubble Bath, Fair Daze, Profane Verse, Trout Fishing*
St. Joseph's Messenger	*Moonlit Sun*
Tale Spinners	*Indian Paintbrush*
Torture and Triumph	*Cupboard Door*
University of Texas Pan-American Press	*Morning, Daylilies, Life*
Verse of the Mirage, 2001	*Norse Viking*
Voices in Italian Americana	*Old Lady with Silver Hair*
Ya Sou!	*Blue Marilyn, Breath of View, Chorus au Natural*

Personal Acknowledgements

I would like to acknowledge all those individuals who helped me during the time I wrote this book. I appreciate all the time and effort they put into this project.

Deep gratitude and profound thanks are owed to my husband, Jim, for giving freely of his time and encouragement during this project. Also, thanks are owed to my children Gabriel, Brianne Kristina and her husband Moulik Vinodkumar Kothari, Marissa Kimberly and her husband Kevin Matthew Franck, Janelle Karina and her husband Paul Joseph Turcotte, Mikayla Karlene, Kyler James, Kelsey Katrina, Corbin Joel, Caleb Jerome, Keisha Kalani Hiwot, Devontay Joshua, Kianna Karielle Selam, Rosy Kiara, Mercedes Katherine, Jasmine Khalia Wengel, Cheyenne Krystal, and Annalise Kaylee Marie. All of these persons inspire my writing.

Thanks also to Madeleine Howeiler, Janelle Hood Turcotte, and Beverly Koerperich for their time in typing the final manuscript and to the team at Artistic Design Service.

Thanks also to the three poets Jonathan Johnson, Marvin Bell, and Doreen Gandy Wiley. Encouragement from their seminars and workshops at Lost Horse Press and Pacific Northwest Writers Seminars gave me the confidence to begin and continue writing poems.

Also, a special thanks to my husband Jim for all the work in arranging the poems and shapes here. I could not have completed this book without him.

A great many thanks are due to my family, who were very supportive during the time it took to complete this project. Your patience and support are much appreciated.

Frost of Spring Green

A Collection of Poetry
Frost of Spring Green Poetry Series – Book 1

Table of Contents

POEMS

Daylilies

Daylilies call out with
  lax, savory whispers.
Fragile free forms: sprightly lemon,
  ochre, chartreuse, and crimson,
wave in carefree meadows.
  Seconds race by and ask their song.

Shy daylilies unfold and reveal the
  perfection of form
enclosed within numerous pods.
  Each a foe of hours,
        friend of minutes.

Only one short day the Creator grants
      to chant a chorus of lullabies,
        thoughts that compel reflection.
  Stems fill the vase with
bouquets of colorful charm that
  languish for attention,
      fleeting color in refractory,
                deep cut crystal.

Carpenter's Daughter

Oak and pine and cedar bouquets
        perfume sachets of wood.
Milky skin, fragrant parings,
        foreign to her nature.
Twilight calls this mind that sleeps
        as hammer music talks outside.
Quiet follows saw blades breaking,
        rusty on the earthen clay.
Splinters fly from the sawhorse that sways,
        trembling on the floor.
Nails pop through the pocket cloth
        of the aging elder's apron.
Sawdust scents the room of the
        sleeping carpenter's daughter.

June Visitors

I watch tiny orbs
    as floral buds swell.
First pea-sized marbles sprout
    then expand to walnut sizing.

All the while the worker ants
    snake on ballooning spheres.
Cycling networks of delight
    Feast on sticky treats.

Sweet feed for their families
    drip down succulent rounds of green.
Buds burst in the moment.
    Petals show off pink satin that unfurls.

Fragrance intoxicates,
    beauty musically exquisite.
Voracious visitors expose magnificence,
    peony ecstasy.

Armies of ants return home
    to feed their families
and defend their farm while
    singing birds prime summer.

June visitors.

Nature's Dance

Hot rays stand above to
penetrate canopies of clouds.
Ever-greening blades of grass,
wildflowers wilt,
bend as music of the cricket chorus
harmonizes with colors
of the sand.

Aspen leaves quake in the wind,
tremble and twirl their soft-shoe style.
Poplar foliage, now goldenrod ground cover,
sways in the distance, as
cattails take their last stand.
All becomes still,
to anticipate the next drama.

Boughs of long-needled pine trees
ripple in the breeze that swirls.
Ice crystals sprout
frosty needles in a glaze.
Pine cones peer through
gossamer-white quills,
to wait for wings to fly.

Blossoms of cherry trees perfume the air,
fragrance delicious to serve a feast.
Hummingbirds ballet on tiny toes and
quench their thirst on vernal nectar.
Honeybees jitterbug in frenzied play
a delight to the spirit,
sensational tonation.

Wine Toast

I hold my sunlit crystal glass,
aflame with the effect
of burgundy merlot
to toast a celebration gift
of life's journey through the
tired face of the corroded clock.

Another salute to the souls
with chestnut eyes and azure
smiles that care.
Crimson wine stains lips
that cannot express.
Cruel and mystical world,
reminder of the velvet,
now-lionized wine.

Crocus

The lovely color of the crocus
   stirs me from sleep.

Petals chill from frosty winds as
   snowdrifts shade early sunshine.

Rain arrives and awakens us,
   Daffodils bud, thick with gold.

Hues of brightness christen others,
   Still quiet in their beds.

Candle Flicker

Sweet beeswax of the candle trickles,
as the fluid flame polishes still.

Darkness smothers the flicker;
it can curl no more.

Dreams of life spiral from the
sleepiness of mind,

In wait of the banshee rooster.
Specks of dust escape all time,

Water condenses on the windowpane,
and seeps down to warp the sill.

Mildew in the tiniest crevices
punctuates the air with the smell of discord.

Ink pen in hand and blank paper,
mellow tacit evening moments.

Oak Tree

The old oak grows slowly.
Yet, she knits such intricate leaves.
Brown acorns befringe
her lap, a harvest skirt.
Ancient oak tree
reaches to the sky.
She dawdles and
strains her arms for

divine connection.
Her trunk accumulates
rings of wisdom,
adding yearly girth. Acorn tree,
for what do you expand?
Your roots branch deeper,
anchor a foothold.
Stretch wider and wider,

search for nutrients,
grasp for moisture,
support the life of
this beautiful matriarch.
Seasons pass;
autumn sets in quickly.
Tired foliage gently falls
into the wind, badges

bronzed and dry.
Parched tones take command
before the oak leaves dervish,
twirl into soil,
and the pulse begins again.
Yet, oak nut tree is not sad,
for winter frost will bring respite,
some desperately needed rest.

Pondering

Eclipsed by the stars,
frightened by the thunder,

stands the moon over the
bridge of the Milky Way.

Lost in glacial mountains,
meadows of beargrass

drip with the crescendo
of emerging battalions.

Armies march in mud to the
call of the black crow's

yellow eyes and sleek feathers.
I summon the souls gone ahead.

They stir for a moment,
then, are silent.

Storm Cloud

He arrives home with
surly arms that end
in strong wrinkled hands.
He stands kind with gentle spirit,
soft-spoken and shy.

A storm cloud then surrounds
him and the room winters.
Slowly, then quickly,
the black raven brings a flurry
that overcomes the doves.

Lightening rage strikes.
Milky skin blemishes.
Sunsets pigment
white porcelain and reveal
cracked vases
on empty shelves.

Wild Garden

Do you remember the view of
that wild summer garden?
Black sweet Bing cherries
hung as tiny ornaments
on the chlorotic tree.

Orchard grass began to brown.
You felt a crunch in clumps
under the soles of your
playful, stumbling tread.

Shasta daisies swayed with
bright saffron centers behind
grandstand hues of columbine.
Honeybees, multi-tasking nectar-makers,
gathered golden pollen.

Topaz-yellow velvet,
quiet under purple,
oh, that summer garden,
I do miss.

Bernice's Bakery

Have you ever driven to Missoula, Montana?
That quaint place in the mountains,
an eclectic mix of cultures.
Academics, aging hippies,
worn-out, tie-dyed,
fresh-faced students
work to earn a mark,
to yield a difference.
All these people, peppered with die-hard cowboys,
old and new, somewhat scarce but can be found.

    Quintessential Bernice's Bakery,
    soaked with the aroma of java
    and ground coffee beans,
    fancy lattes and buttery homemade pastries.

    I prefer the warm spicy Chai tea
    with frosty soy milk.
    Savory spinach phyllo
    melts in my mouth,
    as I watch the wonderful
    brought before my curious eyes.

Lemons

Lemon blossoms
Open, to
Rise with
Morning sun.
Tart
Fragrances
Permeate cool air.
Essence of oil
Invigorates
Senses,
Down their side
While bumblebees
Perform magic.
Tropical florescence
Turns to golden and
Intoxicates fruit with
Yellow prized
Rind balm
Pungent spice,
On sunny mornings
Paints the galaxy,
Surrenders to sleep,
In motionless
Effort left

Birds fly
Over large
Lemons
Dripping
Acidic juice

Honeybees return
to their
Bountiful hives
Deep within
The planet,
Perfumed with
Fresh lemon
Bouquets,
Waiting for
Citrus
Sunset.
Near the side
Of the road.

The Dove and the Eel . . . a Sonnet

There stands goodness in still heavens above.
Picture the soft white dove, icon of peace.
She drives in wind over dew-covered grass
and overlooks waves bordering gray sand.

Evil sleeps below. Perhaps the sky
cannot inspire live roots of sea grapes crawling
to meet blue-green surf. Sea shells line dark shores,
graveyard of conch, destiny of the eel.

Lightning breaks and illuminates white clouds.
Yet, thunder follows, remembering death.
Dove exposes to the slime eel appearance.
Life under earthen ground mixes with sand.

What overcomes deep love of true goodness,
Demons in our souls or selfish desire?

Lady's Slippers

Lady's slippers dance on tiptoes,
Blossoms unfold to morning's
Rosy glow. Shining vermilion illumines.
Chickadees scold young waking chipmunks.

Snapping turtles dig holes slowly,
While squirrels wrestle in old oak trees.
Lake mist rises above the stone wall,
As goldfish circle pink lily pads.

Tamarack boughs edge toward the road,
Which winds through tall cattails
And beckons green mallards
To strut along the spring.

The display ends all too soon
When evening shadows surrender
Sanguine skies, blocked by amber glow.
Midnight covers the celestial sphere,
and all is still.

To Foster

Mom, dad, I want to stay here.
Please don't make me go.
I've lived here over a year.
Don't you want me anymore?

Of course we want you.
We love you and do want
you to stay warm and close,
with our family to support and love.

Then why are you
Packing my suitcase? My
toys? My clothes? Why do
you do this when I want to stay?

My heart is broken. I must
pack your bags. The "State"
says they know what is best.
They say you must go.

And tears run down my cheeks
as go, you must.

Meadowlark

The meadowlark solo is what I remember
To lift my spirits and fill my sails.
Melodious rapture, relaxing trance,
Re-echo across the meadows.

Now I return near streams and swales
to hear the intonation of the lark.
I wait, listen, look at the wildflowers,
but sadly, do not experience the meadowlark.

Where have you gone?
When will you return?
Patiently, I bring my children
to hear the aria I remember from youth.

Yet, I only hear silence.
The quiescence of the chartreuse
grassland now borders asphalt,
cold and black.

Brown Eyes

I remember his toffee eyes,
friendly and warm,
full of life,
looking for fun.
Don't forget the smile,
that Cheshire-cat smirk.

Mischievous,
sensuous, lips
yearn to give.
Encore the brown eyes,
relaxed, affectionate,
ready to love,
to give again.

Memories abound,
his tender chocolate eyes,
soft lips of crimson.
How I miss his smile,
that impetuous grin,
the wish of a tender kiss.

Lavender Visitors

It is springtime and purple lilacs burst.
Lavender fragrance effusive
bloats and explodes.
Action bypasses the

venerable lilac bushes, as cars
stroll down curved lane.
Visitors gaze straight ahead.
Most do not notice spring blooms exposed.

Lilac flowerets strain to get the aliens'
attention, to seek recognition
in the stupor of the day.
Wise grandmother hears the

whisper of the purple-blush
blossoms and notices their tempera
mixed with the motion of time.
Hands on the dial of the clock

abet as the automobiles saunter forward
slowly. Honeybees feast on thick
nectar of the beautiful, fragrant
lavender bliss.

Platypus

Ancient platypus,
Most strange and unique,
You survived millions of years
With your prehistoric skeleton.
Mammal   or   bird?
Teach us   to value,
To respect   nature.
Why class-ify unique beauty?
Freedom is not status quo.
Let the beauty
Of the platypus
Continue to be.
From antiquity
To modern era,
Let's appreciate
The gift of time,
Strange thing
And proud, duck-
Billed platypus.

Morning Pollen

I gaze out my window
and study morning roses,
dusted with pine pollen on
potential velvet petals.

Another mother stares through the pane of
glass, imprisoned with
steel bars. She
looks at a garbage-strewn, squalid alley.

Gilded highlights edge sun-dried pools,
fashion prints lead intensely.
Golden brick road
crumbles in ashen pine pollen.

I smell the fragrant perfume of the
mystical roses that wave
in the flowerpot just outside
my garden window.

She breathes the foul stench
of refuse rotting below
which escapes through the crack in the
door of her sweating apartment.

I send her a bouquet of roses
to place in a kitchen vase. Without
a receptacle, she returns black tulips that
decay to punctuate her statement.

Spilled Wine and Steel Drums

Wine spilled on the lace tablecloth
reminds me of you,

those fine meals we shared
alone together on the island.

We slowly sipped wine as we
savored Flounder Florentine.

Caribbean music serenaded
us in the hushed background of ocean waves.

Fragrant blossoms perfume the air,
sweet spilled red wine, and steel drums,

succulent Frangipani blossoms.
How delightful are the reminders of you.

Betrayed

Betrayed, shocked, shattered,
scattered on the floor,

Cemented together to rise again.
Sweet revenge is what I'm after.

Melt in the kiln,
blue shards of glass,

one giant mass
validates who I am.

Mellow honey balm
fills the fire to the brim.

Molten pot boils and burns
all perpetrators it engulfs,

dulcitude disappears.
Pungent aroma returns

along with bitter taste,
sounds startle the tongue.

Resplendent Morning

Holly-green leaves wave to me
from outside my bedroom window.

Bright yellow-green leaflets
oscillate on sunburst locusts,

framed in purple foothills.
Stately Ponderosas flourish near

dozing, blue waters
not yet awake,

while sunny buttercups
yawn before morning coffee and

stretch one last time,
resplendent morning.

Summer Blossoms

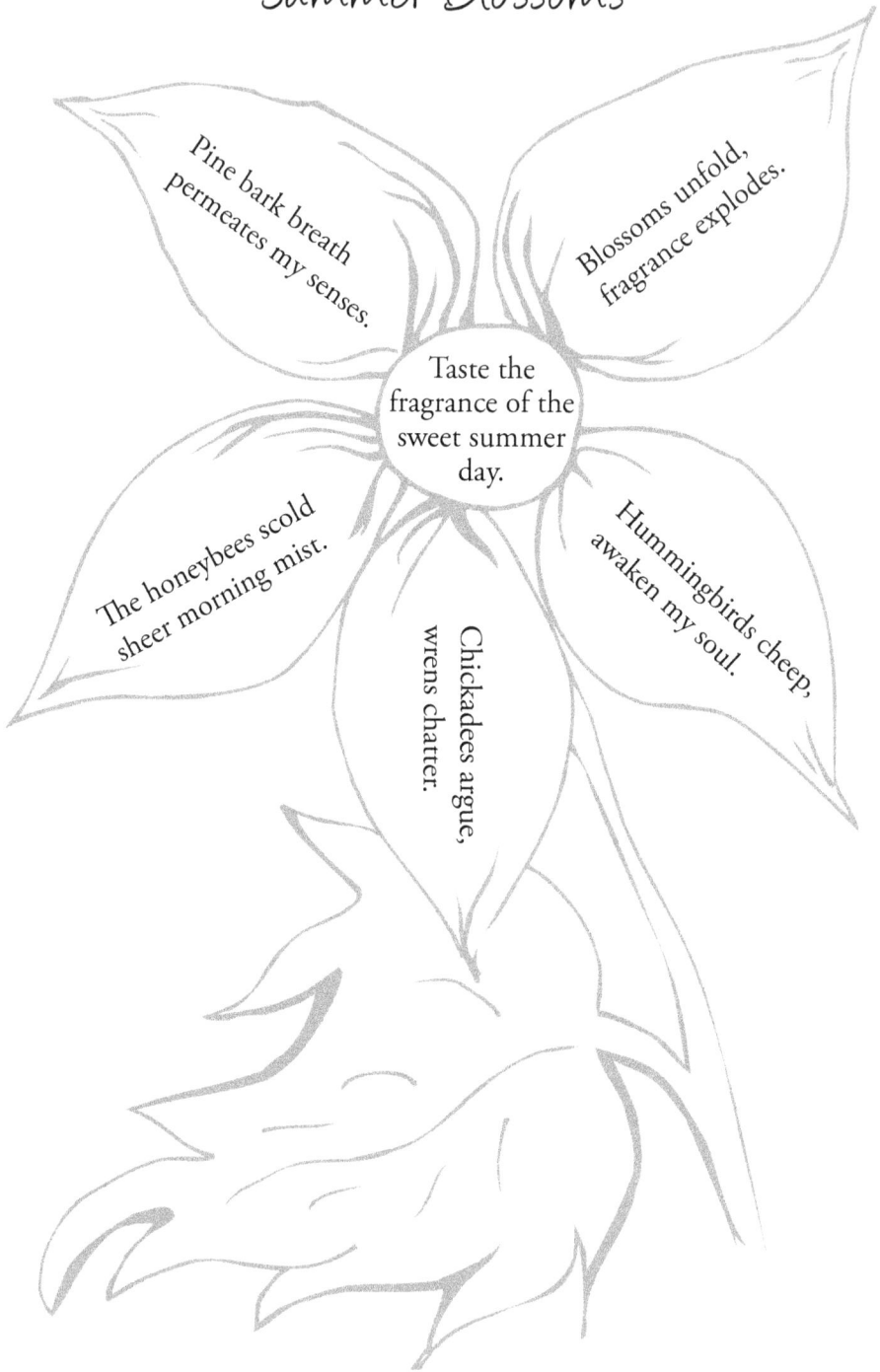

Pine bark breath permeates my senses.

Blossoms unfold, fragrance explodes.

Taste the fragrance of the sweet summer day.

The honeybees scold sheer morning mist.

Hummingbirds cheep, awaken my soul.

Chickadees argue, wrens chatter.

Anticipation

Rosebuds unfold to expose the tender inside.
Dewdrops drip down the vase that wilts, and
freshen the daisies. Behind the glass,
the arrival of baby's breath awaits
the life of spring.

Fresh with frigid waking dew
pine siskins buzz, to
croon with the chickadees, in
pristine frosty air.

Below the Hawk He Walks . . . a Sonnet

He walks among the Ponderosa pine,
Travels deep within the forest green
Where hawks soar higher than eagles dream.
Strength and presence notice, others bypass.
Moon rises, hasty on the blue horizon,
Casts shadows, luminescent images.
As light from stars, sparks above the blackness,
He remembers small fragments of his life
That night below the ever-towering pines.
Often he tries to bury thoughts that haunt.
Now he walks above the shadows that drift
Outside his rustic pine cabin. Lonely,
He asks if eternity comes with doom
or will the pines hide him from such dark fate?

Serviceberry

Serviceberries blossom as
      Telegrams of love that flourish;
   Elegant calligraphy expressed by each petal
      Reminds me of the man I love.

Each spring my beloved gets so excited
      To watch the serviceberries pop
   Like suspended popcorn kernels
      On emerging hills of green.

White blossoms replace the withering snow and
      Trade ice for the warmth of spring.
   Lacy blossoms peek out from twigs,
      Rainy cold still looms.

Forsythia smile their friendly greeting,
      And hummingbirds return.
   Down the road the rhubarb sprouts.
      Daffodils perfume their song.

Muddy fields wait to dry
      As gardeners select their seed.
   Serviceberries blossom on the hillsides,
      Upland fields adorned with splotches of cotton,

      Spring communiqué to my love.

Christmas Cactus

Bright pink blossoms unfurl
Painted with fluted edges,
Enthusiastically open to sing
Beautiful melodies bold.
Vivid fuchsia blooms and flames
As they hang in ones and twos,
Artistic advent silhouettes
Against craggy, scalloped frames.

Christmas cactus stems,
Succulent and old,
Shrivel in spots like granny's face
Yet shout the youth of green.

Blossoms of antique lace distend
With morning sunshine.
Birth of the season, chortling delight,
Friendly with tenderness.

Christmas cactus foliage
Lines my way,
Liver-spotted, yet
Bright and young.

Fair Daze

Do you remember that summer we spent at the Fair?
That hot dusty August when fields lay brown,
Struggling for moisture under the sod that smothers.

Cowboys flirted with me
Standing at the fence, to wait
For rodeo bulls to burst through the gate.

Bucking broncos and wild mustangs
Accepted their bow-legged mounts.

The smell drifted off matted wild horses,
Captured from their native range.

We walked by cowhands
Trying to understand the drama,
Waiting for the excitement to begin.

The crowd roared in the stands.
Weathered gray benches sat,
Bleaching in the sun.

Cotton candy vendors walked their rounds,
As bulls burst forth.
Clowns darted and danced

Behind barrels in skeptical trust.
Rain fell from gray skies
To mesh the dust.

As the final gate swung open.
Rodeo crowds cannonade
And we saw only each other
That sunny summer day.

Juvenile Court

Turn left on Broadway,
take a right on Adams,
there you find the castle
of the judge.

Prison to teenagers,
stark with stares that glare,
silent sallow faces.

A white petal drops, with
growth building on remorse.
You'll discover
courtroom numbers increase,
expansion from our taxes.

Lower levels bring lined beds
assembled in neat rows.
Blatantly absent parents,
stressed-out defenders,
scurry by all-too-busy
prosecutors. New hires
train to pack the garbage.
Who will find the lily blossom
in the mobile alley of darkness?

Laborers

Farm workers toil in the
earthen clay, and tromp through
the muddy farmland to try
to save late harvest. Office
workers scurry through busy
high-rises, working to
make their deadlines. Farmers
and office workers feel alone.
Left behind.
Abandoned and burdened,
humble and in need of prayer,
they are the meek and
humble of heart.

Painted Hillsides

Where are the poppies,
the last rainbow of summer
when petals have
fought the wind
only to lose and be
left as naked globes
of black tiny seeds?
Minute vitality scatters
across terra firma
to wait and sprout
green life in spring;
peasant girls
become new wives.

Remember, Anton? The
summer reds, bright oranges,
pinks and the white that
gave us solace in the
summer from the battles, the
fights, the bloodshed of the
cleansing wars.
We wait for the black,
fine nucleus to serve as
whitewash to brighten
cloistered misnamed
cleansings of
countryside lost in
fields of gore. Tomorrow
the white poppy will
blossom, but the black
raven will abduct
the seed after the
wind rips away
all petals and the
crow will sing no more.

Regression

Multiple regression and hypotheses tested,
Scholars evaluate their facts
Sort, organize, select to find

Data to decorate their graph.
More to plot and verify?
What will the x intercept become
When the y crossing equals zero?

What happens
When life does not parallel
The formula of the lost flower?

Silent Forest

Hush now. You are in the forest.
Listen to the whispers,
the hemlock that tells stories
to the cedar.
Do you hear the legend
of the wind?

Hush now. Stop
your talking.
Each step brings
us closer
to the message.
If only you
could hear.

Somewhere Between the Spice Bottles

There stand the bottles lined in rows,
alphabetically. Parsley,
sage, rosemary, and thyme
should actually be parsley, rosemary,
sage, and thyme, in proper order, after all.
It is the musical tone we favor
and the lyrical notes we savor.

Is there room for tarragon or should
we replace the dill?
Can we find
sweetness between the cinnamon sticks,
tartness within the lemon oils?
Is it the smell of vanilla bean
to prize among the bottles or
simply sweet fragrance that
hides the sour?

Standing Alone

I am a man standing alone,
stoic among tall pines,
longing to board my raft,
to escape the dullness of steel-gray rocks,
silent in the moving stream.

Eagles soar with wide-spread wings,
shadow hidden gold behind hung clouds.
Natural canopies shade sloping shoulders.
Rocky soils trouble worn heels.
I am tired with many miles.

Night falls on thick, pungent air.
Crisp leaves crackle under my leather boots,
while campfires smolder in the distance.
Hawks call to unknown voices.
Owls screech for prey.

I am a man standing alone,
languishing in dormant intentions;
sometimes it is best to whisper
with burning embers warm,
than to extinguish the light in the soil.

Today's Work

Working day by day,
Or side by side, for many years.
Raw humanity in toil and drudgery
Knows and moves with pride and dignity.
Ever-stable was the call of the day
Rigid in moral clarity, our parents.
Scorned by the next generation which sees

    Labor as dishonorable and freedom lacking value.
    Azure blue sky, reflects wings on birds, that
    Change suddenly through dense air.
    Keyboards rather than washboards
    Instant messaging, not patient perseverance.
    Non-traditional jobs the norm; this
    Generation looks for the quick fix.

    Bible anchors find no weight here.
    Another job sweeps broken glass
    Swiftly under temporary carpets
    In an attempt to get things done.
    Can we hold our heads high?

    Even when we run with the deer,
    Though the face of the clock crumbles.
    Hedonistic, tiny pieces lay shattered
    In utter disarray,
    Cheap, disgusting,
    Solitary pieces.

Tripping

Decaying garbage in the city produces stench
that country nostrils cannot breathe.
Vendors sell morsels of fat
drenched in mustard. Crumbs with
salt crystals fall from gifted pretzels,
soft-toasted warm hands of homeless souls
in sunken faces and ashen eyes.
Peanut and roasted chestnut vendors fight.
Raucous noise echoes through dirty alleys.
Moisture seeps through
panes of cracked glass exposed
by the cool drizzle of melting snow.
Skipping down the broken sidewalk, the
hope of running children trips on open cracks.
Skinned knees sting with pain as tears
stream down soiled cheeks. City streets,
home to those without houses, laundry
hangs from covered poles. Street people
long to ride the bus with blurry windows,
a dream,
to return to country life.

Burnt Stones

Somehow five black stones came
inside the rigid eagle,
to wait for their minute to pass
through heavy cloud cover.
Outside floats creation
and blue skies,
white walking stratus,
peaceful in her setting,
green countryside of beauty

One September morning.

Don't call me Ishmael.

After a while dark coal stones
with cores of ice came alive
inside the metal raptor,
working cleverly to gain control.
Boxcutters assume the power.
Fundamentalist fear of freedom
as the soaring eagle
now a missile of carnage
singed by stones, cold of heat,

Misguided crusaders seeking fame.

American souls rise to everlasting peace.

Old Brick Schoolhouse

Aging red brick schoolhouse,
abandoned for time gone
sports window-putty sleep
in dreamy eyes. Doors
yawn with peeling paint.

Townspeople decide to awaken
the slumbering hall;
old and young search hidden
charm. Java brews to
awaken old shutters

and brighten exterior with fresh warm cream.
The brick is given, a brisk morning shower
to brighten aging color.
Weathered gray mortar is covered.
A plaster bath invigorates its tired seams.

Hanging chips of paint are
removed from fatigued entry doors,
which now welcome visitors,
bedecked with shiny brass knobs
and clear windows.

Retired schoolteachers
long gone, now smile
to see mischievous little
bodies enter the once vacant
schoolrooms. And so the
cycle continues.

Ant Hill

Stepping. Walking.
Crushing. Trampling
Human footsteps.
Trudges.
No respect.
No remorse.
Anthills are not
Above reproach.
The ground does thunder
As people crush again.

Cattleya Blossom

Thick waxy leaves protrude
from a pot of bark chips.
Succulent green roots
finger for moisture to
feed the plant that grows.
Delicate colorful blossoms

burst from oval leaves.

Easter Altar

Easter lilies frame the altar,
as pink azaleas lay at foot, with
candle bases elevated.
Flickering flames
conduct the chorus
inviting canaries
to sing in harmony
with warblers.
Bouquets of ebony tulips
meet the fragrant
lilies of the valley
while incense
rises through high notes,
and black
crows pick
the seeds off the
low notes.
Cross and resurrection
one,
redemption,
rooted in
this lived
union.

Horses of Iceland

I looked out the window
Of ice and snow,
Frosted windows frozen shut.
Steam from hot water pipes below
Rises to mist old sills.
It was winter in Iceland
With no sun to shine craved light,
Only timeless darkness
And the eerie reflection on the snow.
More snowflakes fall in sable midday.
It was there out the window
On farmland in Iceland
That I saw my first glowing
Mane, surreal in the
Weather of fire and ice.
Palomino gold, chocolate brown,
Chestnut orange, silver gray,
Blue gruella, and silver dapple,
All with thick shocks of Scandinavian hair.
Steps glide on silky glass.
Gregarious equines virtually magnetized,
A herd as mystical as Viking sagas
Passes like flames erupting
Across the land of pristine glaciers and geysers.
Magical, delightful, dancing movements
Entertain my eyes with
Thunder of hooves, music to
Amuse my ears. In an instant
Horses' tails bobbed from
My view into the opaque distance.
Years later my mind wanders
From a half sleep to remember
The mixture of colors of gold and
Silver combined with murky hues,
Flowing manes fleeing on the glaze,
Those beautiful miraculous horses
Ever so far away in
Iceland, stark and frosty.

Nutcracker

Tears come to my eyes
As I remember the breathtaking dances, and
Polished ballet of the Nutcracker.
Gliding couplets
On elevated toes,
Twirling tufts of pink tulle,
Harmony and elegance grace the stage.
With wonder I do watch
The poetic plot,
Like the story of life.
Enjoy the fluid moments of
Each great, fine scene.
Methodically the pairs float,
Beauty and agility,
Adorn one stage.

Radio Noise

Raucous. Irritation. Blaring noise.
Words that have no meaning.
Percussion and brass offend my ears,
Strange names they give this clamor.

Huge crowds listen to the bellow.
It is for true melody that I long,
Harmony to capture my soul,
Arrest and heal my character.

Mankind yearns once more
To find the symphony
That will mend our hearts
Once again.

See the Glory

I want to share the goodness
of this wonderful world:
truth, justice, love,
fragrant roses, daffodils, and lilacs,
velvet petals and soothing blades of grass.
Fall onto your back
at peace. Look up
at the clouds.
See the glory.

Kant in the Wind

Autonomous moral agent of snow
Talks to the categorical imperative of dawn
and rises in a kaleidoscope of colors.
We are prone to err with the wind,
as we travel in our lifelong search
to follow our informed conscious
before we make our choice.
Choice arises, crisp correctness
or lesser dry righteousness,
or worse. As the wind tears the leaves
from the branches,
the core stands firm, intractable, alone,
anchored in reason.

Embers

Bursting forth in a wave of passion
That awakens the soul
And warms the night.

Glowing embers
of vibrant color,
Stuttering flare.

Embers radiate desolate beauty,
Once alive in flames
Degenerate to smutty charcoal

Left to smolder,
Warming sensibilities,
Hesitant embers.

Latent power
To ignite passion.
Blaze forth hearts,

Remove mankind from cold ash.

Norse Viking

The Viking sat fierce and strong
Eyes of steel and hair the color of fire.
He was going to win
No matter what it took,
Lies, clever cons,
Any measures,
Modern Viking's day in court.
Black robes in the courtroom,
Coldness, hostile silence,
Day of war,
Any method was okay.
Viking warrior fights
To death.
How senseless this campaign.
Can we soften his eyes of steel?
Can we solve this fight
In friendly fashion?
The Norse Viking decides
That honor of domination
Must be defended.
This is war,
And we must fight.
Sadness overwhelms the day.
The battle continues,
Day by day,
Endless.

Mock Orange and Elk

Growing near the verdant hillside
        was a patch of Mock Orange,
sweet and fragrant. Decorating the
        base of Ponderosa pines were more
shrubs of the Mock Orange to mix
        with towering, pungent pines.
Soon the elk spotted the blossoms
        and munched upon the bushes,
a favorite, tasty treat.
        State flower of Idaho and
banquet to the elk, this citrus-smelling
        shrub does serve its purpose.

High Notes

High notes harmonize flutes,
Soprano alerts the butterflies,
Mezzo rhapsody tiptoes,
Blossoming across meadows
Green, with violet daffodils.

Blue Marilyn

She peers
out slatted window blinds
to catch a glimpse of leaves that
quiver, fever-miraged under the sun.
Her eyes beckon one hot August
evening. A lady in blue steps
on the asphalt, heated
to melting noon of fresh summer night.
Silver autos, newly waxed,
drove to miss the
blonde-haired lady who dons
cobalt for her evening
debut. Wind-swept
foliage on fragile stems,
left her skirt above her
knees, where yellow cabs
pass by until
night air becomes stale.
All did wonder why they
watch, as the stares continue,
until the night air becomes still,
yet again.

Desert Dessert

Late one afternoon the cowbell rang again.
A festoon of rowdies marched across the desert

while cactus blossomed in the snow.
Parched earth parted yawning to be quenched.

Sadly nothing more could happen
without the music of the sand

moving down the land merrily as
crystal prisms hung above the sky.

Bubble Bath

She sits in the bathtub,
full of white bubbles that
dance their own rhythm.

She takes her washcloth
and begins to scrub
her flesh, fiercely, then

gently. She grabs more soap
as the effervescent layers,
bubbles begin to fade.

A deviant strain of scum
attacked her body,
invaded her sacred space,

forced patches that rot, to
rob her soul, and created
painful jilts, to her heart,

to kill muscle fibers
formerly alive, which beat
in cadence, of the once-jovial sun.

Mystery Bundle

A package arrives on the
month of frost, wrapped warm
in blankets, a tribute of
knowledge. I open the present
with hands of wonder, spirit of delight.

Then puzzlement overcomes me. From where
came the gift? What am I
to do with this bundled parcel? It
is too large now to rewrap
and put back in the original box.

In my confusion, I
place the bundle neatly on the shelf;
it becomes encrusted again in frost,
outside its warm blankets. I try to
unwrap it again, but there it stands
- a frozen block of ice.

Ever Wonder Why?

Ever wonder why snakes are
      dry and leeches slimy?

Why do bats fly at night
      and birds glide in the day?

How can spindly legs stay warm
      while standing in deep frozen snow?

Why do some people swallow watermelon seeds
      while others insist on spitting them out?

Why did the wooly mammoth die
      frost-whiskered in the cold?

Why did the dinosaurs roam Montana
      where the native tribes later fought?

Why did the earth take so long to form
      and where was humanity all this time?

Why do humans shoot each other
      and pretend only they see?

Latent Knowledge

There she was, sitting
on the table, swinging her
legs back and forth. Olive-
green jumper partially
covering a crisp, white
turtleneck, using arm motions
to make her interjections.

There they were again in
desks too small
to fit overweight bodies
hung on imperfect skeletons
cradling various pens in
left hands or right,
eyes half-open, or closed.

There was the question
on the naked dry erase board
waiting patiently for the
not-too-wet dry erase pen
to print the answer.
Discussion, chatter, silence
then yawned as eyes fell on stained carpet.

Some hair covered brains slept,
while others turned their wheels.
Suddenly, heterogeneous eyes lit up,
white teeth sparkled from pursed lips,
while the marker
creatively colored the board
and the professor turned her head.

Rusting Culture

Cultural machine moves forward.
Small solid pieces weave together,
Moss crawls on heavy stones,
Nucleus still invisible.

Tidal waters exhale only to
Inhale once again, to leave
Barren, salty sands empty,
To dry under fading sun.

Errant species break
Individual encasements,
To shatter molds which
Hold their shape and freeze their destiny.

Lunar energy dusts the planet,
Marks the seashores, protects the tides
Horizontal forces contain the vertical and
Organize walls that hold the ivy.

Beached stones break from boulders and
Crumble, tiny grains of sand,
As pink crabs scurry to hide,
Starfish remain in balance,

Machines of force keep all the same.

Hungry Flies

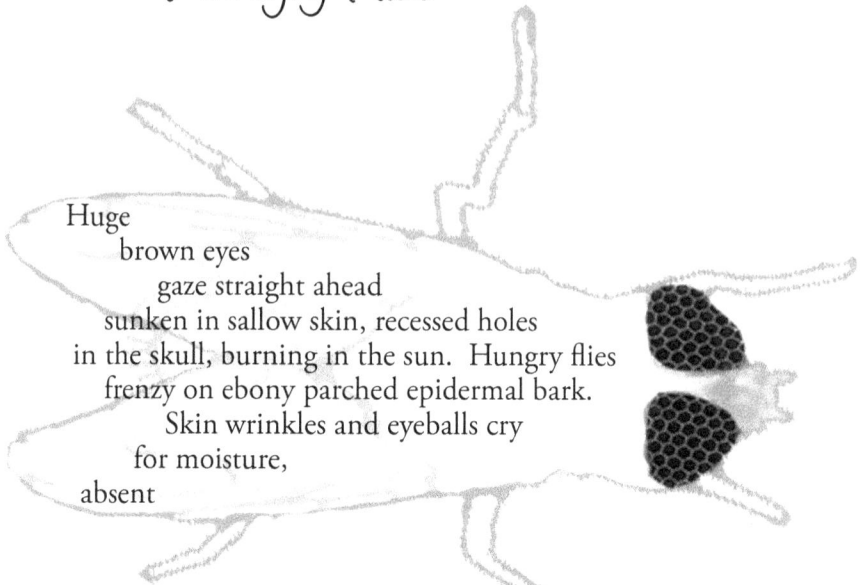

Huge
    brown eyes
        gaze straight ahead
  sunken in sallow skin, recessed holes
in the skull, burning in the sun. Hungry flies
    frenzy on ebony parched epidermal bark.
        Skin wrinkles and eyeballs cry
      for moisture,
  absent

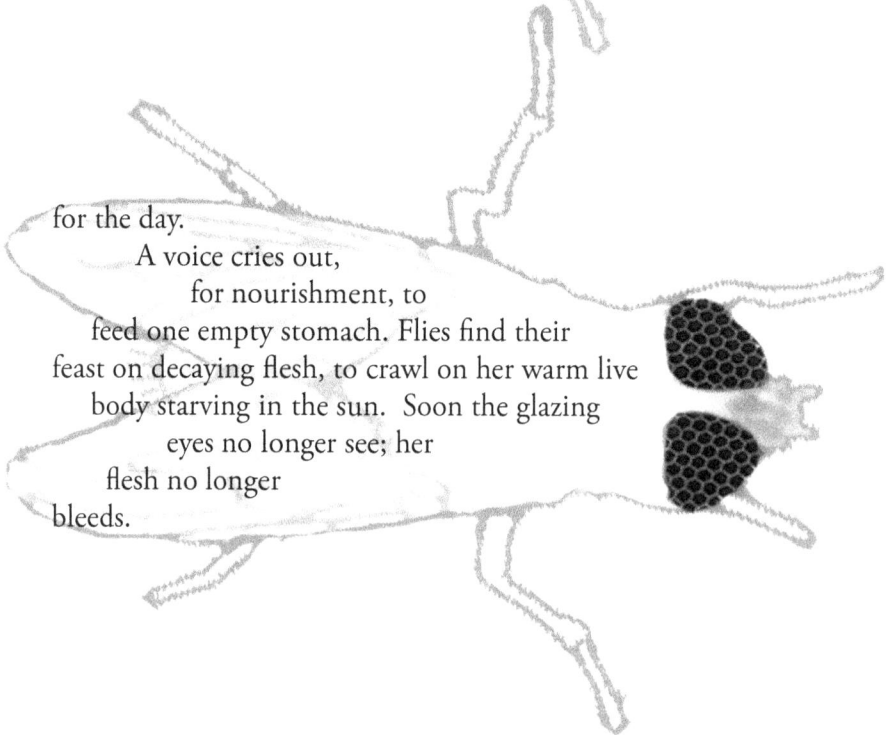

for the day.
      A voice cries out,
          for nourishment, to
    feed one empty stomach. Flies find their
feast on decaying flesh, to crawl on her warm live
    body starving in the sun. Soon the glazing
        eyes no longer see; her
    flesh no longer
bleeds.

Breath of View

Succulent and beautiful, this view
is vigorous marvel.
Everything reflects
original, trusting
as a babe nestles
in mother's protective arms.

Montana Road

Hours I sit as the car
Hums down the endless roads
Across Montana prairies.
I look out smudged windows

Beyond the golden wheat.
Shafts of straw sway in the wind,
Change colors from chartreuse to sand,
Checkered patterns like grandma's quilts,

Squares and rhomboids of fields
Expand for miles.
Alien borders warp along a
Geometric topsoil motif which

Travels farther than the eye can see.
Riding in the car,
My legs grow numb, as I
Sit without moving.

My mind awakens and wonders;
My body dozes.
Stalks of grain undulate to and fro,
Mesmerize me further,

Punctuated by the lone
Montana meadowlarks'
Sweet song. Sing again to
Country Western music twang that

Plays over airwaves.
Vocal rally of
Montana Meadowlarks
Wakes me from my slumber,
They call to my core, and
Pierce through sleeping layers.
Bright yellow breast and black V-necked
Songbird sounds a dispatch

Bronzed in the big blue sky
Upon wheat fields. This bird
Decrees life's message.
Windshield wipers turn as

Drizzle settles dust.
We turn down cracked pavement and
Try to remember the song.
The call of the Montana Meadowlark.

Pavement

On black cold pavement
Look up at the stars,
Hear the yowl of coyotes
In the distance;

Wonder why
We are under the blue moon.
There must be a greater purpose,
For the multitudes to be here.

My heart yearns and
Looks for reason,
Searches for a purpose.
The ache is sharp and cuts to the soul,

At times
Too stifling to bear.
There must be a rationale
For all midnight darkness,

For all those punished with grief and
Vexed with misery.
I am still on pavement and
Wondering why I am here.

What will I do ten years
From now? Will my journey
Be complete and final
Or has it just begun?

I am still confused by all of this
And long for answers,
Hidden dolor,
Mystical answers.

Concealed behind the moon,
Above the pavement
On which I stand.
Alone.

Sleeping Generations

Generations sleep
to wait for death of present,
silent in darkness.

The generation of now presses for change
shining in the future, making
bright lights flicker akin to the flame of the candle.

Forces misunderstood by nature
imprison creative minds spawning
communication in solitary confinement.

The squeeze of newborn children,
causes mothers to look for blankets,
gentle touch related.

Yet, I shiver in the snow-felt future,
generations close their solid eyes
and tech-filled ears locked on forward windows.

One by one the present lives
progress, buried in caskets.
Replication cycles strength.

No creative breaks in molds.

Yellow Bus

I stumbled across a city bus
Stopped and sleeping, hidden
Yellow smudge on acres of asphalt. The
Smell of gasoline mixed with garbage,
Stench of the aged daisy.

At sunrise the bus woke up
To walk its well-worn way.
Doors open, slam shut
On disappearing bodies of
Gazing eyes, sunken in sleepy sockets.

Folding portals release the prisoners
In gray flannel double-breasted suits to
Wait for the crooked old lady
With soiled bags and tobacco-
stained teeth, quivering in her winded rush.

Noon siesta greets the bus while
Snoozing at the stoplight,
Red light glows, warms
The cold vinyl and cools
Urban stench of the daisy.

Supper time arrives and the
Pitch path still needs to be
Traveled by the giant bee
With sooty lettered ads gliding
Across asphalt.

Evening halts the express
And traps sunken eyes
Frozen shut in potholes
And fails to set them free.

Spring Shares

Just a corner of newsprint caught my eye,
Invited me to Sandpoint, Idaho.
There would be teachers and students,
Writers and poets
Walking up and down the street.
Experience conversing with knowledge
While sagacity dances in March wind.
Pend Oreille Lake beckons in silence
Reflects crystal rainbows to
Saw-tooth peaks as friends.
Wisdom sings out again,
This time even louder, and
Whisks my breath away as I
Try to learn the notes.
Harmony and discord
Teach early pearls.
Acrobats drop from mountain trapezes,
As dancers learn their steps.
Forest hikes unfold
Before naked tamarack
That stand sentinel
Always and again.
Spring bounties.

Offerings

Who shall be the ritual?
    The sacrifice?
    The offering?
Who shall grow the healing herb?
    Or sing the transcendent canticle?
We need to find the service,
    the flowers,
    the incense and myrrh.
You can find the wildflowers.
    I will pick the honeysuckle.
    We need to find frankincense,
never mind the gold.

Hooves Pounding

Hooves pound on cold pavement.
Harsh crushing of feet
hamper connections,
habitat not acceptable.

Animals screech, and cry,
out of their element
not in their homes.

Humankind brought to its knees
for ignorance of the past,
careless neglect.

What is left to stand tall?
How can we repair the damage?
The feelings?

Work needs to be done,
to stop the menace of the noise,
The painful noise that haunts,
of the hooves pounding.

Sitting Souls

Hundreds of souls sit in their bodies
on handmade oak pews lined up ever so
carefully at post-Vatican II angles that point
to the altar. Lectors take turns to
read words of Scripture
while minds in heads on souls

try to understand the words
burning toward their ears.
Silently they reflect while incense
floats toward noses attached to faces that
cover minds of their souls.
Eyes bright refract light and

meet with eyes depressed in dormant sockets while
trying to relieve endless sadness.
All look ahead to the cross to
find the path to the switch
that could illuminate the course
that leads to a hidden stance
yet they cannot reach the light.

Arrival

Joy profound announces your arrival.
Your first life breath
Releases in a shrill cry,
Loud symphonies to my ears.

Warm and clammy you work
To seize another breath,
Again, a scream fills the sterile room.
Terror covers your face as
You emerge into unfamiliar air.

Leaving my cozy womb
Must deliver quite a scare.
Hospital workers prod and poke to
Reveal society's first judgment,
An official Apgar score.

Looking out the window
I see butterflies
Rest on vivid bushes to
Herald the announcement.

Echoing time, my gift to you,
Just as you borrowed my body.
Two separate souls bond in life,
Yet living together with plagiarized seconds.

Corroded minute hands brush the
Face on the worn clock,
Primitive numerals beckon silence
Across its expressionless facade.

Grandpa's Cradle

Nighttime dances across my cracked windowpane,
Snowflakes ballet across cold glass,
Frost blankets worn houses.
Chimney smoke bellows in clusters to
March skyward to clouds.

A goodnight story is read,
Lullaby sounds permeate the air,
Hugs and kisses exchange back and forth,
Satin sheets catch my eye
As I cuddle my firstborn.

Grandma's quilt adds extra warmth
As polished red oak
Gently rocks back and forth.
Rhythm of the cantering cradle
Soothes my soul and baby to sleep.

Why the difference among us?
Satin and lace comfort some,
While broken cardboard boxes
Become musty mattresses for others,
Fresh-washed faces shining here and there.

Why should we languish
About things we cannot mend?
My needle cannot sew
Enough satin sheets
To swaddle the cold sting.

Black crows tap at my window,
Calling out my name.
Who will save the child
From the dusky pavement and the
Empty faces?

Who will feed the hungry,
Homeless children ignored?
Who will drive away the crow from
Grandpa's homemade cradle?

Besmirch-Me-Not

A neighbor calls to tell me
All about Fred and Sue.
I couldn't believe the stories,
The awful things they did.

My neighbor did so tell me,
And I told the next three.
Everyone soon did know
The terrible deeds of Fred and Sue,
Until at last…they were dead.

How despicable I feel.
My gossip destroyed
Two very good people,
Kind souls…Fred and Sue.

Old Lady

Do you remember the frail
Lady with hair sky-blue,
Wrinkled and bent from the
Weight of disappointment?

I remember her, too:
Her large white teeth, and youthful
Grin, her crusted, yellow,
and loose, mottled skin.

Closet Conundrum

Closed below hidden hanger of
  Clouds across gray walls,

Should I pick a brown cover,
  Or a black suit? Should I dance?

Warm checkered Pendleton and corduroy on
  Lightweight seersucker?

Save the floral and that
  Herringbone for another day.

What about the brown suede hobble skirt with
  Soft beige cashmere sweater?

With lemon yellow or terra cotta?
  Alligator heels or flats?

Costumes, vestments, wearing apparel,
  Garden clothes with Sunday best.

Sinatra's boots, plush purple boa,
  Silk fitted, or loose plaid?

Striped-thread garb or velour,
  Velvet or grey flannel?

Diamond glitter or wholesome cotton,
  What message is woven in the wool?

Poetry Picture

Poetry syncopates hidden passion of my soul,
Music awakes my spirit,
that aches in my restless heart.
Answers to my questions remain covered.
My journey leads me under the canopy.

Up and down the crooked path,
I look to find the endless meadow.
In the range of wildflowers,
Honeybees discuss the wisdom of life
As they collect sweet nectar

From fluorescent fountains.
The prairie ends below awesome
Peaks surrounded by glaciers,
Moving mountains of earthy loam,
the frame around this endless scene.

Apple Crates

Apple box crates:
Beds or tables,
     Furniture of the Ritz,
        Or storage of the migrant.

Workers in the fields or
     Thoughtful slaves?
       Rough hewn boards build
      Apple crates for export.

Cottage décor and art nouveau lining torn pockets.
     Apple crates stacked with pride by
       Calloused leather hands
       Seen by sunken eyes.

Feast or famine, red or green,
     Brown hands rugged for the lilies.
       Blossoms unfolding or
       Wandering weeds?

Rolling Palouse

Lush green rolling
Hills, decorate
Basalt
Outcroppings to
Irritate
Productive farmers.
Lentils
Talk to
Lost goldfinches
Seeking home.
Wheat fields
Plead their
Perennial case to
Agrarian economists.
Tired souls
Glare
At rain
Reflecting
Green tractors that
Glide over worn gold, to
Scream for
Measured sunshine.

Barefoot Girl

Barefoot girl, stands
With strands of gold,
Eyes of sapphire.
Garnet lips,
Cry out in darkness.
Dying honeysuckle,
Wilting blossoms,
Feathers floating,
Till all does
Touch the ground.

Hauser Lake

Azure-blue lake,
Silhouette of mountains,
Cricket music in the wind,
Pine trees release,
Wildflower kaleidoscopes.
Fragrance of fresh-cut grass frames the
Dilapidated cabin.
Windows begin to tilt,
Only to meet
With neglected deck,
Overgrown with moss and
Dishonored by geese.
Mixture of pleasures,
Nostalgia and quiet wonder,
Continue to drift at
My lake…Hauser.

Frost of Spring Green

Frost covers the pines
with eloquent gossamer frosting,
crystalline ambience.
Yet, with this quick-freeze delicate
comes the icy anguish of
beggars on the street
and homeless people,
youth discarded, absent mothers,
fleeing fathers unable to face the
reality of the day.
Foster systems overcrowded,
home-finders stressed and calling.
Around town, snowflakes flutter to
ask if anyone has an extra bed.
Flurries blast and crystals
form to capture prisms.
Jeweled tones reflect the
new waves of
pristine snow,
hiding the weeds upright
from showing their non-white souls.
Blankets of frozen, whitewashed cotton
hide the frenzied blackness of the city's
spirit, as the meth kitchens cook
their soup. Frenzied druggies
make their buzz, while
tear-filled babies' eyes cry with
total wonder, and the crank
junkies stew more highs.
Snowflakes float again
as a lactescent blanket,
an unnoticed patchwork of
stumbling stories,
abandoned adolescents,
and pillowless street people,
calico children with no beds.
Butterflies heed the warning
of the green grass of spring.

Tamarack

Crisp orange air,
Autumn needles that crumble,
Brilliant rays stream.
Sun ablaze,
Moist breeze,
All waken my spirit.
Tiny golden blades
Dance to the ground
From pendulous twigs,
Defoliating my favorite tree.
Now naked tamarack
Mirror my soul of
Many dormant colors.
Valued by Native Americans
Fibrous tendrils
Entangle broken basalt,
Tenacious.
Divine rays
Awaken my character,
Nourish my soul
With misty breath
As needles fall,
Leaving the
Wardrobe-changing tree,
Stark and hopeful timber,
Bare to the soul.

Wrapped Packages

God announces the truth of creation.
Sky blue displays divine function,
In waters of oceans and lakes.
Sometimes we forget to thank.
We do not see the

Package adorned so perfectly.
Ideal gift wrap stretches out far and wide.
Ponderosa pine trees cloaked in long, deep-green,
Fragrant and aromatic, refreshing Tamarack
Dressed in needles changing with the seasons,

Lush verdant thick in summer,
Disrobed in winter.
Blue swift skies decorated with
White fluffy clouds, that shift with the gift of wind
Stars twinkle, as eyes sparkle in darkness.

Autumn Air

A bountiful autumn
Arrives rather early,
Cool crisp air
Warms maroon colors.
I yearn for its approach,
To draw close to my chest.
Strong and mighty autumn flees
As quickly as it arrives
Leaving me cold and empty,
Arctic cerulescence.

Glacier Stream

Sitting on a boulder bench
The glacier made for me,
I gaze across the sky-blue lake
As ripples wave to me.

Looking down the wind-blown water
The aspen leaf turns up.
Its broken stem caught
Within the stony swill.

Leaning down, I clear the leaf
To travel down the stream
Free to complete life's journey,
To course along the shore.

My gaze turns back again
Out across the lake,
To view the glacial mountains,
That capture my beating heart.

Clouds touch alpine heavens,
Ice peaks, majestic
Frame basal basalt, rocks
Almighty memories.

Velvet Rose

If the luxuriant rose is velvet red,
    what is the fragrance of today?

When the petals wilt and drop
    does the rose's naked center miss them?

When the roots reach out for water
    will the stem be thankful?

Complicated, savory, rose red,
    I breathe your sensuous texture.

Sidewalks

Desolation lingers
    in dark streets,

People pass
    others disappear into mist,

Walking skeletons, pallid eyes
    stare into emptiness.

Art galleries with broken hearts
    echo images subdued.

Flowers need paint,
    while houses scream for comfort,

Graffiti-muraled walls,
    foibled concrete vestments.

Dismal lights glow,
    mulling cardboard beds.

White hair covers worn-out circuits
    engaged to the moon.

Broken bodies display curly locks that
    lie in melancholic shadows.

Crossroads, ponder which path to take,
    while aged sidewalks crumble.

Oaken Planks

Raised grains of sun-bleached oaken planks
Lie beneath my calloused feet,
Weary from days of work.
Prints unfold to read as tea leaves,
Mapped in hardwood below each cracked sole.
Deep pain felt with each new step
The mighty oak tree weaves a tale, to
See eyes of time recorded.
One hundred years of mighty pride,
Producing acorn's providence
For generations of squirrels
Eager to devour each tender morsel.
Golden leaves spread to dry ground
Swirl down parched souls.
Wait for the winter frost and
Thorny thistles dance across the oaken casts.

Sanctification

Breath of life presents a gift,
Image of God dwells within us.

Respect hangs onto a black abyss
As humanity shares the looking glass.

Crowding in the center,
The race of man pushes

To get a better view,
In vitality's enormous mirror.

> Levitical religion:
> Sanctification not salvation,
>
> Thoughts restrict access and behavior,
> Pattern clarity from wonder.

Love stands present,
Sometimes a dying trace.

Hatred grows tall and
Shades the fragile flower.

Embarrassment brings a flush
To warm reflected faces,

As we are awaken from sleep,
Dazzling semblance.

Actions echo,
Budding relationships

Unfold holy bouquets
To share.

Conception

My life began
at conception.
Simple cells,
sperm
and egg, unite
to create
new life
unknown.

Mystery of
deep ocean
bloom
swells warm
within the womb.

Soul and
body
blend,
spirit deep,
wet darkness.

Energy of life
precious
becomes
a shadow,
yet unborn.

His Eyes

I felt his presence in the room,
Powerful, palpable presence in the room.
Ogle of his dark brown eyes,
Staring at me in the room.

A glance, a brief glance,
Is all I would give
As I walked through the throng
In the now-claustrophobic room.

I often wonder,
If I paused,
And stopped, and looked,
And gave him back his eyes,

If that would cause
A transformation in myself,
A change that would turn about all time.
Instead, I vanish from the room.

Night Whistle

Do you remember that
Hot August night?

Iowa humidity so dense
You could backstroke in the breeze.

As mom and dad new, we came home with
You, back to our tiny apartment.

The brassy train whistle
Pierced our silence.

One quiet night with you, now
Dead within my body.

My beautiful dark-haired
First baby boy, still.

The last long night
I shared together with you.

Autumn Glow

Autumn appears. Ruddy glow shimmers
over crisp air. Pungent aroma
wears afternoon apparel,
noisy in the wind.

I am a basket of maple leaves
florid and crinkled with age,
scalloped from an artist's hand,
one more powerful than words.

I snuggle with the oak leaves
much smaller than myself,
golden in color. I nestle with the acorns
strong and majestic, leathery and sullen.

I imbibe the heavy moist air
euphoric with nature, rolling in the sun
to watch over rotting pumpkin vines
blind-sided by the snap of weather.

Life's basket will give me rest.
while others may perish.
Dark tiny apple seeds and tough acorns
lay waiting, to germinate and
grow once more.

Huckleberries

Small, dark, violet berries cluster on the bush.
Fragrant, delectable berries ripen to burst.
One by one, slowly, over the summer season
huckleberry leaves form a tapestry
on the forest floor. The palette
blends its colors over mountain slopes which
rise to peaks that touch white clouds.
Pickers travel many miles to search.
Purple bounty, tucked under forest canopies,
hides in rugged alpine terrain. Each pair
of hands work to fill their bucket
of pure royal stash valued by
those that crave its mountain-
berry flavor. Regional pride takes
over as each keeps his or her wild patches
secret. No one wants to whisper
where they find their sweet, savory
violet gold, distilled juices packaged
perfectly on the bush. Jewels of
lividity hide under Northwest sun.

Cupboard Door

Her face was pigmented sunset,
Vibrant amber, rose, crimson,
With some purple mottling,
Some splashes of midnight.

One swollen eye surrounded by
Warm beige makeup to tone
Down some of the brightness of sunset,
A pair of frosty blue sunglasses
Perched on crooked, feminine nose.

Her familiar fresco looks more artistic,
Yet frightening to behold.
"I walked into an open cupboard
Door," she said.
"How stupid of me," she said.

Yet we know how intelligent
She is, and beautiful and kind,
Not careless enough to walk into
A cupboard door again . . . and again.

The hues of the sundown will
Slowly fade from her face,
But with the dark circle of midnight,
She will continue to live

Until she finds
The courage to face away
From that old swinging
Cupboard door.

I Love You

I love you more than beargrass,
        that blows in the wind.

I love you more than daisies,
        that undulates in mountain meadows.

I love you more than glacial streams,
        that fall from sunset cliffs.

I love you more than the blades of grass,
        that wave in soothing breeze.

I love you more than azure skies,
        that drift across tall mountains.

My love grows far beyond your words,
        written on the page.

My love for you is beauty beyond perfection;
        joy completes my craving.

Dear Daughter of Mine

Dear daughter of mine
Beautiful eyes, a
Doorway to a kind soul,
A heart that trusts,
So much love to give.
You gave your love,
True and sincere,
To the love of your life;
You thought.
You planned to share long years
Together with your love.
Sadly, plans abruptly changed
As your "love"
Betrayed you.
Pain and tears fill your heart
And now you deeply grieve.
Misery as dark as death.
How I wish I could lift your anguish
And bring back your carefree smile.
Many times I think of you
And yearn to wash away your sorrow.
You are good and kind.
It is a mystery to us all as to
Why you have this burden,
Inflicted only, because you loved.
Loved with such a trusting heart.
I know not why this other heart
Betrayed you with such malice.

Please know that you are loved,
With all our hearts;
And these hearts will not betray
Your love or trust.
Also know that this will pass,
Like gray clouds in the storm that
Drift away in darkness.
Once again the sun will shine
And sparkle on spring flowers.
You will then wave goodbye
To dark and gloomy storms
That hung deep within your chest.
Stars will trip again the light fantastic
And twinkle in your heart.
Yes, your soul will glow again
And rejuvenate clear sky.

Rain Clouds

Why are rain clouds black and fluffy
And dry clouds white,
Erratic in the sky?

How can there be a black cloud
Stuck in the middle of cumulus delights?
Why are white clouds so thick and downy?

Persistent farm workers
Toil in ebony soil below, worn hands plant crops and
Wait for the ominous cloud,

The single black cloud to
Release its rain, water the soil,
Soothe the blisters on wrinkled hands.

Tired workers bring bounty to our
Tables where we sit cozy,
Comfortably warm,

Not even aware
Of the story of the black cloud
And all its vital rain.

Meaningful Eyes

Eyes forward, and then
A glance.

Bashful eyes back forward,
And then another glance,

This one longer
Than the last.

He put his arms
Around her,

Held her tight,
Then tangoed

Along moonlit shadows
Left by others.

Shyly, she chose the lemon
And stripped its peel,

Revealed with coy,
Sour flesh.

He selected pomegranate
For its inviting ruby layers.

She enjoyed the taste
And dripping juice.

He unpeeled
layers and folds,

Separating plump seeds
And reddish taste.

Together they clung
And quivered and tasted

Till there was
No space between them,

Only darkness
And sweet perfume.

Winter Skies

Gray winter skies,
Crystal-coated pine trees,
Majestic blue mountains
Complete the Northwest frame.

Altostratus clouds drift downward
As another sky border
curtains celestial regions.
Snowflakes dance a lullaby,
Then sleep under moonlit heavens.

Trout Fishing

Early dawn rings the bell,
As trout fishermen
Rise to follow
Curbed riverbeds, wise with stones.

Azure water, resplendent,
Curls down straight
Pathways hidden intermittently
From golden sun.

Excited anglers walk
Between mountain cliffs.
Trapped fossils struggle in
Murky creek beds,

Glowing over russet gems,
Messages in the sand
Wait to be found,
Like notes in ocean bottles
Long lost in tidal seas.

Shimmering rainbow trout,
Mimic the majestic
Skies after sopping spring rains.
Tails frolic in the cool mist of
Bubbling green-blue waters, to

Cast dancing shadows
Under glittering sunset gnats,
Who tell their story but
Are silenced by the wind.

Profane Verse

Crude words abound
interwoven in daily
conversation,
to punctuate sentences
throughout all verse.
College-educated
mingle with
grade school dropouts
using short, disgusting
utterances, to enjoy
shock sensations.
        Just as redundant use of "wolf"
        pares down peril's perception,
        profanity becomes mundane
        hearing insults all day,
        on the street,
        at work, and in
        music videos.
        New movies disappoint,
        narrow word stock on display
                Listeners grow
                weary of terse
                vocabulary
                spat upon
                naked senses.
                My soul longs for
                melodic verse
                written in musical
                fashion. Phraseology,
                with lively lexis,
                is what I crave.
                Unique coloratura.
                        Eggplants and
                        strawberries
                        blossom
                        in the garden
                        pollinated by
                        honeybees exposed,
                        serenading
                        messages in
                        soft fragrant
                        breezes.

Ocean Waves

Tropical ocean waves crash and
Fall onto sun-bleached shells.
Frothy crests brew in strength
Till they force their way to boulders
Framing the seaside shores.

       Salty smells mix with
       Malodorous fish to punctuate the
       Stinging breeze that tickles my
       Sunlit face.
       Hermit crabs crawl by carrying

Their houses far-too-large, as they
Conduct their work of
Today, while a baby eel strays and
Struggles to find its path through
The maze of rocks aligned on the shore.

       Scuba divers line up
       To pay their dues, exploring
       Unseen ocean floors, modeling
       Their newest gear. A barefoot
       Native woman walks

The burning beach
With her net, to find
The caught flesh of the day.
Everyone goes about their business
Yet, they do not see the sand.

Casket

I wanted to
feed her thin
blue wrinkled body
shrunken with pain,
an apple.
Alas, it was
too late. Instead
I helped at
her burial,
kissed her lips
and closed her casket.

Alpine Mist

She stands and looks over the lake one day
And wonders out loud about creation.
There it stood in lakes and streams

Surrounded by glaciers so proud,
Always melting, not quickly.
Rocky mountain goats.

Climb the ragged distant rocks in measured step.
Indian paintbrush whispers back and forth
In cool gentle alpine breeze.

Hoary marmots whistle and
Beg mere morsels.
People overfeed in acts of kindness,

Visitors realize not, the damage they have done.
Earth and environment slip away
In each moment of time.

Small Blur

Walking past the slate of glass
A glimmer stirs my field of vision.

A whir, a flitter, a blur of color
Mixing heavy air, to

Search for nectar droplets
Trickling down petals, heavy with fragrance.

Hummingbirds iridescent hover
From flower to flower.

Acrobatic movements seldom seen
Delicately fast-forward in mid-sky.

Tenacious, fragile beauties,
Wondrous joy, for but a moment.

Autumn Snow

Why does autumn bring the snow
When summer drops the ice?
Waiting for the veins of henna,
Crimson maple leaves,
Odiferous moldy acorns
Provoke fuzzy gossamer
To package pungent aromas.
Spicy apple astringent,
Warm cider pressed, ever
Punctuated with the fragrance of
Pumpkin seeds roasting in the oven,
Cinnamon spice,
Vagabond leaves
Crunchy in the snow.

Restless

Tossing and turning
        under flowered muslin sheets,
I want to sleep,
        and enter that blissful state.
Instead, my mind alert
        slowly signals my eyes
To open and breathe the shadowy darkness
        and exhale past dreams.
I struggle to view the clock
        to find the exact time,
The crazy hour.
        Again I tell myself I must sleep,
I hear the tree frogs outside
        loud in chorus to the wind.
The bark of a stray dog
        intrudes upon amphibious melody;
The fresh smell of May lilacs
        brightens the view.
Usually this interruption of my sleep
        Would ladle stress upon my conscience,
Yet tonight the incursion tranquilizes.
        I enjoy the two a.m. serenade of tree frogs
Accompanied by the wind, and
        punctuated by the scent of lilacs.

Fragile Hands

Big blues with dark curly lashes
stare across the room.
Fragile hands, elegant fingers
wait to be held

by someone who loves.
Instead, the hands hang limp
next to sunken sides,
then fold shut

to make an empty fist.
Lullaby, my sweetheart,
don't you cry.
Why the blank stare,

that drifts from
those peacock blues?
Whisper still some more;
talk again to my spirit.

Such melancholy lenses
uncover my inner soul,
lead me to you.
My eyes connect with yours

while heaviness presses
against your chest.
Purple tulips wilt
while yellow daffodils bloom.

Chokecherry Syrup

Deep crimson mason jars lined in rows,
Carefully sealed golden lids,
Collect dust on uneven birch shelves
Trimmed with yellow paint that peels.

Old, worn hands cracked with age
Squeeze berries picked before.
Chokecherries hide behind olive leaves
Framed in carmine gold.

Search that brings
Fond memories,
Bind up our belongings
In the old blue Chevy.

Drive the stick-shift
Down the road,
Up to the foothills
Below Montana's Rocky range.

Right by the road
We stop,
Papa, Mom, and me,
Look through the

Myriad of verdant bushes,
To find small burgundy berries,
The old, bitter, beautiful
Unrevealing chokecherries.

Ode to a Rainforest

The flower of beauty,
Spring,
Soft
With lavender petals.
Fragrance as
Sweet as vanilla,
Pollen dripping
From majestic
Trees in the rainforest
Disappear
To the cities.
Mankind
Cuts tall timbers
For treasures
To line pockets
Of urban dwellers,
Destroying
Nature
With clouds of mist that
Hang over
Decaying
Stumps of
Timber.

Palm Sunday

Five weeks of Lent and then it is
Palm Sunday.

Thousands of people gather in
Groups on the worn square, to

Wait for yellow palms that
Border citrinous green.

Palms fray at the edges,
Emit fragrance of immature fronds.

Children stand in line and
Wait for their strands of golden green.

They wave yellow strips that
Sway in cold breeze,

As cleansing rain
Patters down over repentant crowds.

The throng teems forth and sings out
Together

Praises their Messiah
With honor and respect.

"Prepare ye the way of the Lord,…"
sings out the tenor.

Melodic voices follow him to the church
Where the sorrowful congregation

Honors their Lord, and
Pays homage to Jesus.

Grief remembers the end and
Waits for resurrection.

Rain drizzles and stops its sprinkle,
Sharp wind penetrates bones.

Eyes stare forward
Retracing what happened, and

Try to salvage meaning
Now and here.

Callous Colors

Fragile, old, yet vigorous,
Marie walks outside to pick the iris.
Gaudy headscarf adorns her bald head.

Respect she shows to the fine iris as each
struggles with scarred petals, in the weather.
Now they stand together, strong.

Cancer has taken over Marie's bones,
while the hailstorm ravages
fields of iris blossoms and they remain proud.

This sixty-year-old lady is far too
young to succumb to nature;
iris blossoms, as gallant flags,
reassure her.

Marie glances as the
crystal twinkles,
purple iris in its prism.

Butterflies stop to
kiss the harmony,
gentle in the breeze.

Slowly the sun
fades, to bring
final rest for the
kind zephyr.

Tempered

I wake up to the sunrise;
       It is night.

I go to bed at sunset;
       It is morning.

I lay in the sun;
       It is winter.

I roll in the snow;
       It is summer.

Season my soul with vitality,
       Tenacity, the truth of my bravado.

O Beautiful

Do you think the rose blossom
would be as beautiful without its thorns?

Would the cactus flower be as exquisite
Without the prickles of its stem?

Would the honey locust beckon still
Without its tree of barbs?

Beauty and bramble grow together;
Velvet to soothe, and thorns to bruise.

Can we see the beauty
Without ugliness?

White souls
Without black?

Truth
Without lies?

The brilliant bluebird
Flies with magpies,

While the canary sings
With the hyena;

Frolic engineered in the snow,
To rid itself of darkness.

Long-needled Pine

Crowded pine trees
Over stretching mountains.
Forest with cinnamon bark
Beautiful in my view,

Gently boughs sway
In warm breeze,
Nothing more restful
Than the fresh fragrance of pine.

Memories created,
Family moments
Preserved in history in
My long-needle pine.

Little Walls

Stark white walls line narrow stairs
That lead to the counselor's office.
Little children, ages two to four,
meet with their mentors, to
try to diagnose problems and
find the source of their
pain. Mysterious ghosts
exist within the confines of
these nurseries.
Ghosts
Didn't hug them.
Didn't make them feel safe.
Now Johnny and Susie stare in
blankness as they walk
past vacant walls to
counselors. Their advisors
cannot smile but
continue to paint
hallways white;
the children live
in windowless blackness.

Canvas Depth

She looks into the painting
to see shades of blue in the lake.
Suddenly she is sucked into
whirlwinds of the palette below the
surface of the canvas. Rich in texture
coarse brush strokes are hidden,
the artist's limning.

She gazes up from under painter's cream
that spins from the funnel.
Pigments separate the swirl.
Finally, all becomes clear and
there is no mystique that remains.
Stars glimmer above lakes,
crystal water cries for respite
from the overactive artist. Her
imagination cannot rest.

Feminism

I was always proud to say,
No feminist am I,
A women's libber,
  Definitely not.
  No association with those bra-burners
Did I want. I feared them.
A bunch of militant activists on a rant.
  No, a feminist I was not.

But why? Women oppressed:
For thousands of years there's been
Spousal abuse, battered women,
  Occupational segregation,
  Pink-collar workers, no child support.
Women survive adversity,
Limits on their freedom.
  The hierarchy of most churches of

Man do not acknowledge their parity.
Why are behavior and rules disparate for
Possessors of the feared wayward genitalia?
  Women are sexually mutilated in Africa,
  Sold into slavery in the Far East.
Female circumcision scars
Innocence of women in Egypt.
  In China and India

Baby girls are killed,
Justified they say.
After all…
  Many traditions have patriarchal legacies
  And the soft, gentle, fair, weaker sex is discarded.
What do we do? Those of the second sex
Deserve to stand on the same level.

Women have inalienable rights.
Women hold up half the sky.
Of course, I want to fight
The hobbling effects of
Injustice, unfairness,
Physical abuse,
Fundamentalism,
Mental death.
I have always stood strong

On issues of human justice.
Therefore, I must rethink
The feminist label I cast aside.
Who made "feminist" a dirty word?
It is consistent with all that makes
America indivisible in its liberty.
Alas, reality is exposed.
Engagement is imperative.

The label can unite efforts
And make all strong.
Not separation,
Not abortion, yin,
Exclusion or isolation,
Feminism is true democracy, a web-like
Praxis, a mentor's spirituality, a
Powerful cultural victory, an

Often-misappropriated word, a
Civilizing influence, an
Ever-evolving wholism. We are
They. Yes, indeed, a feminist
I will gladly be,
For myself and others.
In fact, a feminist
I have always been.

Wrinkled Gardener

The furrowed face
Upon the man
Gardening with his wrinkles
As he plowed the land.

I watched this wise old soul
Sow his seeds by hand,
Then studied the liver spots
Upon his freckled forearms.

His back was curved and matched the face.
Countenance of the man haggard and worn,
Full of wisdom of years gone by.
Understanding as he stroked the ground.

He seemed to whisper to the soil,
To know the wind,
To listen to every reverberation
Expressed by the soul of the earth.

I wish I knew what was said,
What Mother Earth told this gentleman.
Instead, I have a novel unanimity
Of the detail
In the gardener's face print.

Score of the Pine Boughs

Look up at the pine boughs
Musically swaying in the summer breeze.
Listen to the woodland song,
Study the lyrics in the melody.
Learn from the message.
Wonder why the journey of life
Is not so harmonic.
The chickadee flies above the boughs;
The wren is angry.
It is the goldfinch song
That will win
The tune of victory,
Synchronized with the
Score of the pine boughs.

Motherly Gardening

My mother
Taught me
To garden,
To dig with bare hands
In clay and
Loam,
And crawl with
Montana angleworms,
That shine in dim
Rays that reflect
From Big
Sky. My mind
Wanders
Through the muck,
Reddish heavy,
Muddy ooze.
Intrigued with
Life
And worms,
Those bugs
Slink through
The gumbo,
Slip
In its
Heaviness.
Great Falls' gusts
Remind
Me to
Plant those
Seeds
Before Chinook
Winds come
To make
More mud.
Wise old mom
Knew that
Earthen mire
Grounded me
In ways
Earthworms
Inch and
Always
Understand.

You on My Walk

We had been apart so long
   I always dreamed of you.
   Finally, I went on a walk
   One day and looked off
    Into the trees. There down
   The path I saw you. Your
  Height, your shoulders
 Your dark chocolate hair,
 Your agate eyes. I became
Warm with excitement
And to you I ran, to
Hug, to caress, to kiss.
 Only he was not you
 And my face wilted with
   Disappointment as the
    Smiling goldfinch flew
     Away and brought back the
    Bluebird.

Neighbor Boy

I can still
Hear the piercing
Screams today.
The five-year-old boy
Down the street
Crying and
Wailing
As his mother
Continued to
"Spank" him,
But I knew it
Was a beating.
She was out to
"Teach" him a
Lesson, to be
A "good mom"
She said. I
Can hear yet
His cries from
When I was ten.
I can even feel
My sick stomach,
This very day,
From that "good mama."

Autumns

It is nightfall.
Out of the black sky,
Color fills my soul.

How many autumns
Will my winter life be long?
All day and tonight?

Why does the bud live
When the spring blossom dies?
Suddenly cicadas sing

In my rest this night.
I hear the flowers visit
While earthworms are still.

Lilac Hammock

Lilac blossoms intoxicate
Unfold on the borders,

May blooms long-awaited.
Wooly bumblebees pollinate

With their yellow coats and warn
Neighbor honeybees, work

To make thick golden syrup
Lazy in the morning sun.

Bright orange ladybugs
Stroll across verdant leaves.

Chestnut-breasted robins
Chatter in the distance,

While vivid green tree frogs
Chirp unseen.

Breezes soothe and transport billowy clouds,
To shade sunbeams from my face.

Hammock sways in the wind
Between favorite crimson maples.

This moment returns
With every lilac visit.

No Restful Peace

Bundled in my bed,
Ever so cozy and warm,
I snuggle between my soft blankets
And silky sheets more.

Don't make me face the world today
I can't bear to see
Gloom and sad headlines.
Instead, I'll nestle in my bed.

Today's news I'll not see
In the safety of my covers.
I'll cuddle, rest,
And hide again

To enjoy . . .
Immunity
From distress,
In my intimate nest.

Blaze

A fountain of petals,
Red, burgundy, velvet, crimson,
Layers cluster together.

Flower fragrance drifts,
While spirals unfold to
Uncoil from one tight center.
Ladybugs move among the network of branches
Covered with thorns.

Stems arch upon green stems,
Buds continue to swell
Until they burst forth.
Spectacular fountains glow red,
Cascade over pendulous branches, that
Bend, tired in the radiant sun.

Honeybees swarm upon sweet nectar, which
Drips of essential ghee.
Hummingbirds engage with wings that swirl
And dart within the tangles to take their drink.

Wellspring of Blaze blossoms
On the maturing rose,
Respite from random business
Of the non-productive day.

Indian Paintbrush

The paintbrush of the Aboriginal American
Jostles in the glacial breeze,
Before my eyes with awe,
Imbues legends of mystery and wonder,
Portraits of rose, rust, and burgundy,

Enlightenment unfolds for the ancient and young.
The tradition of the native brush strokes
Decipher the lacquer of folklore
That sways in the wind.
Roots below the soul reach

Deep within the craggy burl.
Local bare and scraggly branches
Crumble to the universal call;
Intrinsic whispers shout.
Working honeybees stop and strain, to

Listen to the paintbrush,
Thankful for the deeper maxim,
Wisdom of the plant beard.
Finally, the mythos' secret is understood.
Mythical children smile and wave

Back to their fellow tribes,
They carry the tincture of wisdom,
And the wind does rest.

Yesterday

At nightfall I grow weary,
And it is time to rest.
Thoughts grow in importance
As my eyelids begin to close.

It was yesterday when I was
A new innocent soul in my mother's
Arms. I enjoyed pure air
And sweet milk.

Today, I struggle among the clouds:
Sometimes white cumulous
Other times gray storm clouds invade
And taunt with occasional blackness.

I yearn for the twilight of yesterday
When all was quiet, soft and clean.
Today, dismal clouds stifle
My vision and breathe my air.

Awaiting

It is you I see in the cerulean sky.
There, in the long-needled pine,
I wait for your return.

In the evergreen shade, I remember
The long soulful walks,
Jovial tunes,

Skipping along lake shores,
Sapphire blue,
Dark as sunrise.

Silver Reunion

Muggy air, dense and damp,
Not usually encountered.
Wet blouse baptizes my back.
Steamy sunglasses perspire, and
Block my view of the misty lake.

Feelings rise from places unknown.
Memories and scents of the past
Puzzle and question my sanity.
Movie clips of days gone by,
Scenes from film repressed

Long ago. Sounds parade and,
Colorful pictures
Awaken my ears. I recall
Humectant thoughts.
Overload returns as antique black and

White movies of twenty-five years ago
Rekindle Benedictine memories,
Reach my spirit. My experiences in Minnesota
Revive as I sort out time.
Four years spent in the land of 10,000 lakes,

St. Joseph, St. Cloud, and Minneapolis,
Enriched my soul and invigorated my spirit,
Deeper than life's days, that pass.
Faces painted in the attic of my mind.
Dusty cobwebs,

Transformed by two and a half decades
Form a collage and window to my soul.
Will the window lead
To a door, or simply thick cement?
Painted dark colors protect the visitor hiding within.
Silver-topped faces are sorted to view the exquisite beauty.

Old photos recovered and antique picture frames,
Memories spritzed, revisited.
Northern Midwest landscape echoes time,
Senses of beauty surpass memories,
Temporarily suspended in passing moments.

Feminist Label

Roses and marigolds,
tigers and lions,
dance with butterflies,
skate on desert sands,
divided by cracks in
parched soil.
Dehydrated roots
wait for raindrops
to blossom again.
Where are women afraid
of the feminist label?
How do men scorn
the word?
What is a Feminazi?
Why should the voice of feminism
frighten the fair-minded,
the loving, the kind,
the powerful, or weak?
When can she decide to become
a stay-at-home mom,
or not?
It is her choice to select a career,
or not.
Feminists are independent-minded
and seek justice for all.
Feminists are influential,
thoughtful forces of change.
No burqa body bags,
nothing to fear or scorn
or undermine, have we.
Relish the uniqueness of
man and woman. Appreciate
snails and puppy dogs' tails,
intermixed with sugar and spice
and everything nice.

Awake

She knew fear and could not sleep.
Fear became her friend,
The one she talked to in the night.

Poison filled her body fluids
And threatened to drown all lights.
Nothing could silence the songbird,

Nor the music deep within.
She began a journey with her
Comrade of night

And learned the function of her escort
That beat within her soul.
Not the beat of a drum. Instead the

Drum of percussion that crashes on brass,
Lacking notes, no rhythm in
frosty summer air.

She trained her new partner to
Resonate warm waves. Soon
Fear became a comforting quilt,

The sound of the curved creek
Running over uncertain rocks,
And finally she could sleep.

Storm

Looking up we saw
The angry, violent skies.
We felt cold and helpless
Listening to the storm.
We knew it
Would be over soon,
Our bodies
Shaky and shivering.
Our journey
All too quickly
Ended,
Much too early.
Down the path
We ran,
Before we too,
Were white and still,
Blue and chilled.

Sweet Peas

Pleasant memories embedded
In sweet fragrant blossoms,
Piquant incense,
Fruity yet spicy,
Peppery sweet,
Perfume for the senses.

Cave

Know that the secret is buried
Deep within the cave, far below
The hands of time, that shine
On ancient sundials, crooked
With the mantra of the twisted winds,
Making tunnels in the sand.
Look for a master to know
The answer as the stranger
Passes by and dispenses
A cursory glance. Wait to
Hear the solution
Sought within the lair.
A channel weaves its way
Through the grotto in the
Sidewalk's dampness. Crystals
Grow longer and more pointed
Adding stalactite sagacity
As well as carrying mysteries,
Message too difficult for mortals to decipher.
The mountain's weight smothers
Ceilings trying to crack the dark,
Dripping cavern's hidden enigma
Undecoded. Copper and silver
Mines remain elusive, solemn
Stone, subterranean secrets.
The roots of pine trees burrow
Below patchy meadow rock
Hiding tempestuous treasures.

View Out My Window

Looking out my window
    Watching buds unfold,
Rosebushes need pruning
    Lawn in disrepair.
Excited to begin the day I
    Rise and toil in fresh earth.
I want to do everything;
    I want to do nothing.
The goldfinch remains elusive
    As rhododendrons stay in bud.
Creeping phlox sneak past me,
    While bleeding hearts throb in the wind.
I cry for time to stop;
    Instead it continues to betray me.
Time refuses to listen
    And speeds on.
Only once I blink and the rhodies are gone,
    Waving to magnolias,
While baby's breath cries out
    For tender care,
Only to languish again
    In cold soil.

Unquilted

I tuck my
children in
toasty beds,
to say
their prayers
under warm quilts
like I used
to do
when I
was a
child.
Only now
they ask
if they
will
breathe
anthrax
from unknown places
and die
like the
people
in the
newspaper.
Their quilt
cannot hide them
from the news.

Fog of Darkness

New jobs available, posted,
groups needed for the bust,
give a call, no, three or four,
report the strangeness.
That eclectic neighborhood house,
curtains drawn, lawn of garbage
smother spring flowers that
struggle to blossom,
dead cars scattered out back,
boxes of empty cough syrup.
Bottles confuse the huts of
rats biting foreign objects,
spreading their disease.
Visitors push the broken doorbell
rusted, closed with the warp of time.
Doorbell replaced with knocks on splintered
wood, once held proud as castle's
doorway. This time squeaky
splitting doors open to guns drawn
and uniforms covered in prophylactic plastic.
Sunken eyes are banded in wrist
shackles without looking back to
toddlers in fetid, fermenting diapers
sitting listless on lice infested couches.
Then depressed eyes cry out for
food, long for clean spring air.
Dampness of the morning must
be replaced with salty tears.
Meth fumes cloud the air
and the music fog
of darkness plays forward.

Twinkle of Your Eye

Your chuckle makes me smile.
Your laughter brings me tears.

The twinkle in your eye
Is mystery for my soul.

I long for your embrace.
Your loving arms

Surround my heart,
And merriment dances once again.

Your voice I hear, although a whisper;
I long to feel your breath.

Violet Aster

The tiny violet aster with lemon-velvet center
moves its heavy head to and fro, up and down.
The aster tries to bid me to listen, to stop and heed.
Instead I rush right past its face again

I do not stop to attend.
Later that day, I remember
The tiny violet aster
And the pretty lemon center

Of the personable purple potential posy.
How it strained for my attention
Swaying up and down,
But no, I would not listen.

I walk back to find the violet aster
To take some time and enjoy
Its darling face and yellow center.
Alas, it was far too late,

The dainty aster was no more.

Pine Cones

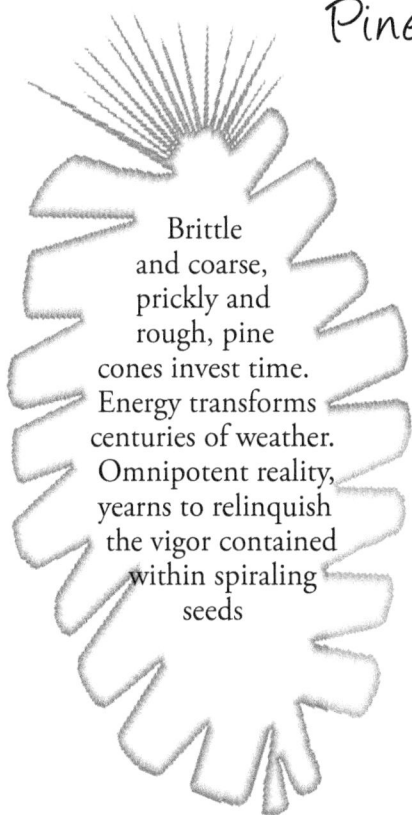

Brittle
and coarse,
prickly and
rough, pine
cones invest time.
Energy transforms
centuries of weather.
Omnipotent reality,
yearns to relinquish
the vigor contained
within spiraling
seeds

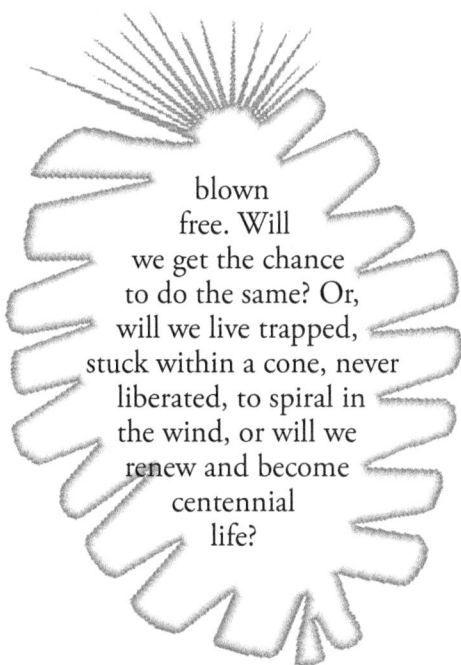

blown
free. Will
we get the chance
to do the same? Or,
will we live trapped,
stuck within a cone, never
liberated, to spiral in
the wind, or will we
renew and become
centennial
life?

Uneven Spirals

Snow blizzards waltz across
   tropical beaches and grains
     of sand. Sunrise sets in the black
      of midday; evening brings warm

      frosty air. Arctic winds toast the
     frozen bodies that bathe in
     glacial sand. Fatigue energizes
the weary, rising in the

morning dew. A hummingbird
   knocks briskly at the window. A
    rose-covered bungalow
     is lost in glacial

     snow. Honeysuckle perfumes
    dusty air. Mermaids float over
   ocean floors, while children skate
slowly on desert ponds of ice.

Circular spirals gyrate
   in motion; russet leaves embrace
    bright lemons. Huckleberries blossom
     in the sun, shining on cactus flowers in

     frenzied flurry. Fresh scent of hay
    mowed, falls on curved black
   pavement, surrounded by
skyscrapers, lining towns

of ghosts. Rhododendrons sprightly
   unfold; tamaracks aprons itself with
    gold tinsel. Each stark stick in the forest
     serves its purpose, timber of

dry barren soil. Mountain ash fruit bursts
forth; bright orange berries gather
dust. Evening grosbeaks sleep
until sunset glow emerges

in the dark. Steel energy hot
as ice, molten lava sprinkling
forth, spinning leaves falling
up, as spirals change

the creek. Waves balance on tight
ropes, crescent moon hangs
on a string. Apple wood burns
amber, ignites the cast iron

stove. Dull cardinals fly
in tandem. United brightly colored
sparrows fill the starlit
turbinate; tired wings rale

into darkness. Eyes fixate from minds
mesmerized. Swirling butterfly thoughts uncurl
the spiral. Stark cold flashes, spring warps
curled ribbons, and straighten
impotent coils,
uneven spirals.

Cardboard Hut

Young girl within the honeysuckle
hides in a hut of thorns.
Her soul illuminates iridescent light.
     How she loves to sing.

Dark brown eyes of deer and lips to match
the mulberries on worn branches. Cheeks
the color of rose flush in crimson sunset.
     How she loves to sing.

Yellow daisies kiss the fall dahlias,
then turn black after the surprise frost
brought with seesaw winds.
     How she loves to sing.

Soon the frost turns to chill. Raw
gusts inaugurate the frightful blizzard that covers
the hut of thorns; the cardboard folds on the street.
     How she loves to sing.

Street sweepers push away boxes,
hands tear down the hut of thorns
until asphalt shines stark and clean.
     Now she longs to sing.

Pollen Beyond My Reach

It is clover sweet, that
Intoxicates deep within my soul.
Spice scents fill mind
As bees collect their gold.
Light glimmers between the blades of grass.
It seems that dusk will not fade the
Joy of morning's dawn.
Fear reproaches my tender spirit that
Yearns to eclipse the awe of light,
Inkling that feeds my spirit.
No nourishment so rich
Can move my soul
Than pollen beyond my reach.

Life

Innocent babes
  Within warm womb,
    Dark and febrile,
    Wet and cold,
      Nurtured by

Their mother's body. Later
  Suckled warm maternal milk,
    Fresh with pheromones
      Only baby knows.
        Gentle arms surround this infant,

Knit a blanket of stitches
  That knows no time.
    Lost below the sky,
      Red sun rises
        At midnight,

While the moon
  Appears in blue morning,
    Sleepless from
      The night before to
        Wait for the breast to dribble.

Breath grants life's sweet milk.
  Suckling in the soft
    Breeze, as time courses
      By, slowly.
        Life moves forward.

About midday the baby calls
  For lunch and learns the wisdom
    Of the day. Light becomes the
      Wind and storms.
        Sunshine rains in the

Dry desert sands,
  While ice forms on
    Lavender-chilled moon
      Far ahead.
        Skewed horizon reflects

Honeysuckle in the meadow.
  Distant view are muddy and thick with
    Heaviness of smothering air.
      People gasp in search of the
        Essence of life, only to

Be disappointed to
  Find autumn air.
    The mystery of life is there and now.
      It is hidden, circling as a tornado.
        Winds spin around wheat fields and

Hide quiet peaceful
  Center, concealed in the eye of
    Dark angry winds.
      Destruction of life
        Within its path.

Starlit crows argue with
  Beautiful bluebirds brilliant.
    Daffodils fight with the crocus as baby sits to
      Hear rose petals dropping on the asphalt.
        Fragrant lilacs profess

Control of the swarm of bees that
  Try to silence the singing
    Canary. Baby falls asleep
      In nurturing arms. Mother
        Awake and weary.

Sweet Clouds

No air to breathe anymore.
clouds I inhale to quench my thirst,
give me strength.

Bluebird songs I do taste
to give me nourishment,
become my food.

More children are homeless
today, crying in pain;
fewer parents will take them.

Not many adults show care.
Who will bring these
Abandoned, our anaweim,

home to caress, to nurture,
to love? Sedaca announces
directions on guidance.

Instead we turn our gaze,
shop for more toys,
line our walls with things.

Together we smell the sweet clouds,
inhale and intoxicate
ourselves, so we can see no more.

Chorus au Natural

Ethereal beauty breaks silent air
  As dulcet lilies direct the chorus and
Beckon alto hummingbird voices
  While tenor doves resonate natural mystery.
High-pitched shrieks of the eagles alert the
  Golden swallows;
The song of the meadowlark sings a breakfast solo.
  Patrons sit in upright chairs and
Wait for the duet of the flautists to pierce the air.
  Daffodil heads bow in respect.
Narcissi are more impatient to take their turn.
  Sunrise sets and dusk does fall;
Chorus of nature bares
  The timbre of the quiet sunlit night.

Servant Woman

She walks barefoot; hands
Hold a silver platter
Upon her head.

She walks proud and
Full of spirit, even
When her feet grow fissured and weary.

Tall woman displays ebony skin
And warm brown eyes
And proud posture.

Her hands and feet
Aged, cracked
And wrinkled

Beyond her years.
We order off the menu
And she serves us standing

At the table.
Scrumptious foods,
Wonderful spirits

Fill our table. Drinks imbibed
And then, lodge in my throat
Unable to swallow,

Haitian servant
Slave to tourists
Mother of nine.

Montana Hometown

Big sky is loved in the Montana
hometown in which I was born and conceived,
the place of the golden wheat oceans
reach out and lap the tall mountains.
I visit again and watch all changes in the

City of Great Falls home of the
Russell Museum, the display of
Western art. We celebrate history and the
time of Lewis and Clark.
Chinook winds stir brazen wheat

stalks; breezes move in waves across
expanses of fields too large to embrace.
Farmer's field stretch out to touch the mountain base and
frames the city of constant wind.
It is the area of eighth avenue north

at twenty-third street that I know best.
It is this place that overlooked the smokestack of the smelter
on the mighty Missouri, as the water roars through the
valley.
Yes, it is where I was born and raised;
the place I owe my spirit.

Moonlit Sun

How long will be my life?
I asked under the sunlit moon.
It seems I want to trade
My days of the magical
Worker bee with the giant
Sea turtle to bask in the
Hushful moonlit sun.

Sand Castle

My love, king of the outdoors
Lion and leader of the jungle,
I love to see your kingdom,
Twinkle in your eye, light in your soul,

Harvest from your open hands.
Crushed shells and sand between your fingers

Yield rays of sunshine as
Flowers bloom in rows.

Your shovel will turn more soil and
Crumble between strong hands.

Take grains of sand to build my castle,
Lost, time to love again.

Mask of Layers

Take off your mask, dear love.
Your shiny, painted, beautiful mask.
Tiny flaws and cracks
Hide lacquered layers to
Reveal mundane colors.
Colors that wait to come alive.
Peel off the arrogance and
Throw it on the glass pane's
Windowsill. Leave it there
To rest so I can see
Your fine sullen eyes. The
Windows to your soul,
Asleep in two caves.

Bluebird Beckons

The bluebird beckons me
Down the trail to
Follow this first-prize ribbon.
Staccato waves,
    I watch;
Gentle breeze,
    I feel.

Flutter and frolic,
Summer bluebirds sing
The melody that beckons me
Further down the path.
    I wander,
To watch the fleeing royals.
    I see.

All is still.
Fragrance of bright
Spring blossoms,
    I smell.

Breath deeply fills my cup.
    I drink.
Dew saturates my skin,
        I taste.

Alas, the moment is broken.
The scolding of the wren hastens.
A step in the rhythm of time.
    I hear.

    Listen.

Toast

Blown crystal glass of wine
We toast together,
And share the fire
As we sit side by side,
Eyes long for each other,
Parted lips,
Finished wine.

Patchwork

Across the rolling Palouse, we rode for
Hours and hours. We gaze
Over incessant landscape that unfolds to
Monotonous plains.
I wait impatiently to see the
Arrival of the Rocky Mountains.
Wheels rotate over streaked
Asphalt. Uneven
Patchwork patterns
Camouflage old potholes.
Windshield wipers hum to
Background radio music and
Awaken our sleeping senses.
Down the winding rutted road
We travel . . . and try not to slumber.
Alas, I watch the driver,
While the cracked windshield
Fades into
Dusty breeze.

Sigh

She asks to see
        rosy amber colors and
Rays of sun streaming to break the
        Morning mist.

She asks to feel the succulent
        Bright yellow daffodil open its
Scented buds and unfold
        majestic, perfect blossoms
On healthy stalks of green.

She asks to hear the songs
        Of meadowlarks, loud
And beautiful solos across the
        Grassland.

She asks to taste
        Sweetness; instead, she
Can only smuggle and swill
        Alcohol.

She longs to smell
        Volleys of fragrant
Hyacinths clumped in
        Meadow grass under her exposed feet.

Instead, she gapes at
        Darkness, gray
Clouds, and drizzle.
        The trees stand bare,
And their fallen leaves moldy.

She could imagine only magpies
        Feasting on remnants and
Hyenas laughing as they feed on the dead.
        Her vision is blurred,
Yet she cannot witness the decay.

Pike Street Market

Crowded street,
Excited throng,
Bluebloods and bumpkins
Push through
Vendors.
Delightful colors,
Aromatic bouquets shout.
Musk of music runs
Through droves of
Energetic vision.
Fresh fish fly, to
Argue with clams and
Land on ice beds.
Songs echo from below while
Ponderosa pine needle bundles sit
Next to rhododendron blossoms.
Kaleidoscope of colors
Paint sunrise palettes.
Shades of skin
Pyramid luscious fruit.
Strands of gold
Cross Seattle's blue mist.

Different ethnic
Dialects harmonize,
Rhapsodizing
Drum beats of
Wildflower honey.
Washington Salmon struggle
Upriver as butterflies bask
In the morning sun.
Fresh-baked
Pastries
Quell
Short tempers.
Daffodils dance
With the blue moon.
Pierced and tattooed,
Artists and poets
Vocalize as the
Flautist performs
Till crowds
Drift asleep and
Paint the
Sun emerald.

Mantel Clock

Amber moon
rises over the moun-
tains. A   glimpse
of silver   sheen
spotlights   the rug-
ged cobalt   horizon. A
smile awakens   your face. I
hear a brogue within. Romance and candlelight
two-steps with the symphony of wind. Soothing melody caresses my ears. I
gaze into your caring eyes; bouquets of floriferous freesias complement the
evening setting. The brass clock on the oak mantel stands silent, rests but
for a moment, centered and still.

Despondent

She once lit up the house with her sunny smile,
flashed her beautiful white teeth, and
danced with majorette kicks.
She once was healthy and full of giggles
ready to share her joy.
She picked bright-colored flowers, and
placed them in fine porcelain.
Today she shows sunken eyes,
swollen skin.
Now she picks black tulips
To wilt in a mason jar, as
pollen dusts down the glass.

Who is Out There?

Is it the fragrant pine
or yellow buttercup,
that sings to
silent chickadees,

Who is out yonder
across the meadow
that stands tall,
alone?

and calls to noisy crickets that
sleep under lilacs
with the tree frog
chorus? Ripples

cascade across still
ponds, as lily pads
carpet rippling water
in silver patches.

Amber air meets
dark crimson clouds,
wrapped crisp
around the moon.

Aspen leaves quake in
bunches to rustle in quiet
evening breeze, while one
alone does quiver.

Brown stiff bark curls
Around the tall white trunk
that grows and struggles,
then begins to shed.

Who can say the
conductor dozes
when the symphony
no longer sleeps?

All speak their own
music, carried in
midnight songs
blanketed the dusk.

Elk

Our search for mountain elk begins
in darkness before dawn.

Midnight shades undercolor still,
turns tones of amber crimson,

as hues of the sunset hang on the distant
horizon that follows shallow creek
beds. The stream turns between the hills

that frame. Soon my eyes fall on the
first elk of the day. He stands
yonder on the edge of water
and golden tamarack.

In silence
I stop, and pause and
take a moment to inhale
this pure view. Thankful for

the bounty before me – elk
and mountaintops,
creek waters, wind,
and all falls silent.

Sunrise at Forest's Edge

Sunrise brings crimson rays. Pleasant warmth
reflects on blades of meadow grass. Blades
stand upright and hug brightly polished buttercups;
purple fleabane sways gently in cool breeze.
Music of green tree frogs echoes softly.
Playful butterflies frolic
sweet. Love sings songs only I can hear.
Collage of songs reveal yellow canaries,
while bluebirds imprint dark silhouettes below.
Inner circles spiral from old pine cones.
Fragrant pine needles stifle thoughts.
Tall ancient trees sentinel before us.
Love withstands the soul's rhapsody and
takes breath with every limb.

Circles

Earth's rotation brings us
Wonder as we spin in
Circles. Arcs surrounds
Us as our lives
Whirl out of focus.
No beginning while
We grow. Leaves twirl on
Circular twigs. Pinecone
Spirals announce infinity,
Spinning, circling, never ending.

Lily Pads

The lily pads grow intertwined and
Weave a mat of leaves outstretched.
Ripples, waves, currents baffled.

Pianissimo haven for tree frogs to
Sing and promenade on pads.
Water lilies abloom.

Painting pastel pigments;
Food for silent spirits,
Soothe clean souls.

Amphibious
Archipelago

Adrift.

Meadow Music

The music of meadow grass outside
my cabin window wakes me from
my
      nightly
slumber, far too loud are the brassy
flowers. Intermixed with this percus-
        sion.
I can
hear
the
verdant
green
of grass,
exhale
in rest
from
their
musical hymn.
Boisterous roots toss
and turn to find comfort in
dense thicket. Sleeping earthworms
awake annoyed with raucous noise
while ebony crickets punctuate night air.
Gregarious buttercups share their evening news.
Giant toads dominate the chorus; hornets
hum irregular rap. Finally the blade
of grass, as a conductor's baton,
silences the others for a mo-
ment. Still as a Buddha.

Glacial Beauty

A woolly marmot pokes her head from the
Canopy of wildflowers.
Purple-petaled fleabane drifts in cool breeze.
Don't forget the textured palette,
Soft, warm glow burns sorrel.

Shaggy Rocky Mountain goats
Peer from behind rugged stones,
Saw-toothed edges, and craggy-cliffs
Reveal their home.
Subalpine clouds crawl to reach
Pinnacles and whisper to the
Meadow grass's
Single blades.

Bird Woman Waterfall
Talks in the distance as the
Weeping Wall cries below.
Cedar paths display mossy meadows
As bristlecone pines struggle to survive
In the alpine expanse.

God's canvas of colors mingle and
Kindle deepest embers to
Bring magnificence and
Visit my humble spirit.
A grateful human I am,
Witness to this glacial beauty.

Wintry mist refreshes
My face, vision beyond belief
Fragrant meadow wildflowers
Begin life's dance.
The sun does rise
And all do sing.

H o m e b o u n d

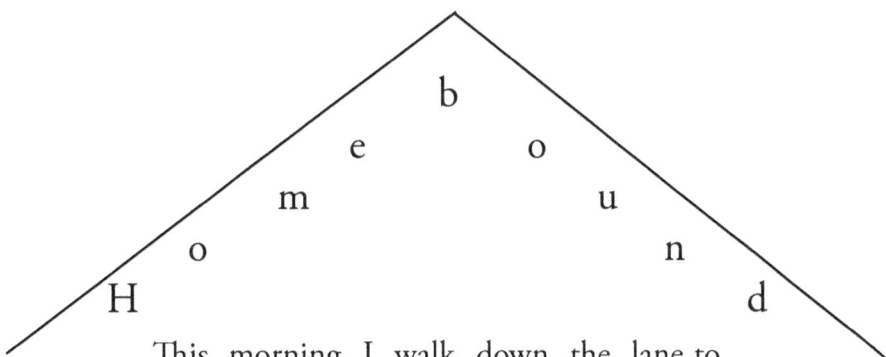

This morning I walk down the lane to
our red-trimmed, white house, topped
with scar-let tile to take
a divine breath of the
magnifi-cent air.
Inhale the distant
clouds that greet
me from the blue
sky. I put on my woolen sweater and walk
to the rose garden, full of multi-
color, aromatic petals. I
cut a succulent branch of
thorns, and savor the velvety
blood blossoms bursting
from their buds. I pause to sit
on the worn arbor-covered deck that slopes,
while hummingbirds con-tinue their ballet
through pendulant fuchsias that drip sweet
syrupy nectar. A feast for
these jubilant, hovering
wonders. Tiny bards in flight
to Mexico rush before giant
snowflakes make frosting
on the trees. The monarch
butterflies laugh with yellow
daylilies before the final
biorhythm of the day.
All is mystically forever fragrant.

Gray Spring

Eerie is the spring storm that
Brings gray skies in sudden motion
Over rumbling blare.

Thunder cracks and startles us
After lightning strobe-lights
Ominous skies.

The worried robin reads the message,
Too obscure for humans.
Birds strut with russet breasts,

Wings take cover in the nest.
Heed the tone of thunder.
Humans busy about their work

Scurry in the dark of day,
Make sure their techie tools
Keep productive through the bolts.

Robins try to relay their message
Received while they brood over eggs,
Musical notes not seen but felt

This autumn day in spring.

Horse Delight

Craggy mountains cast silhouettes
Over the still azure lake;
Sun shimmers within the distant glow.

Green rolling meadows dense,
A carpet of radiant plush
Soothes my steed's tired hooves.

Wildflowers blossom while
Bouquets of bluebells
Fidget in fresh forests.

All echo melodious
Pictures as I ride
Down the curved path, and

Enjoy the crisp
Wind on my face,
Only my horse and delight.

Greening of Walls

Outside…the city is green,
from blades of grass, while
floral artists ornament dim landscape,
yellow with daffodil blooms,
alabaster with fragrant paper
narcissus. Cherry buds
unfold on dwarf trees that swell,
succulent with nectar.
Birch bark peels and flutters
in brisk spring breeze.
Lemon-toned warblers sing
angelic music, to await monarch butterflies,
mosaic patches of pigment
lush with gentle wind.

. . . . . .

Inside….stark white walls freshly
painted line the stairs to crowded
rooms next to each other
with doorways stacked, like
rungs in a ladder that lay down
as a gateway to this monochromatic maze.
Gold doorbell chime and red door
opens to allow the child visitor
to enter. They sit and chat
with sunken eyes and solemn
faces. One hour they talk
in stoic language without
words, somber exchange
of glances, adult and child.

. . . . . .

In between....the therapist records
daily trauma, the nightmares, the
physical abuse. Inside, the child
halfway recounts the horrors,
then runs through bleached-white
corridors to cry in the
colorific landscape. Rain
washes the lurid spectacle
in torrents,
until there
are no more
tears. Only
stained
soulless
hollows.

Haiku x 10

Blue winter morning,
lactescent blanket snow white,
doe, spotted fawn, run.

Bright autumn sunshine,
lazy sunflower heads droop,
scarecrow, silent sleep.

Brambles dense thicket
shrubs hide thorns, dense verdant leaves
brown rabbit escapes.

Gray chickadees sing
Long-needled pungent pine boughs,
rain mist dusts night.

Daily enjoyment
pink rhododendrons blossom
cool spring dawn arrives.

Divine radiance
young bluebird feathers shimmer,
blues morning rises.

Bright mustard, field sprouts,
sun glimmers in night blue sky,
fall meadowlarks sing.

Hummingbirds flutter
over bright fuchsia blossoms
falling in night wind.

Ponderosa pine
Shelters groups of chickadees
Under fragrant boughs.

White cumulous drifts
carefree children dance on stairs
gossamer landings.

Little Blue Eyes

The doorbell rang.
My heart did leap.
Little blue eyes
peer through
window panes
of beveled glass.
The red oak door
swung open
with such anticipation.
Two sets of blue eyes
sparkle, effervescent
in the morning sun.
A strawberry-blonde
drops into my arms;
she looks confused
and a bit concerned.
Her stares penetrate in my eyes
as I look into her soul.
In that instant my heart beats
to grow in love once more.
These inner eyes of blue
stir my spirit to palpitate
and remember, those forgotten.
Her weak smile so shy
warms my heart.
She was here to stay.

Rest

Can you find the robin's nest
Hiding in the magnolia?
Milky white petals
Cascade to make mish-mash.
Cotton candy swirls of clouds,
Soft as baby powder, frolic
Together in spring breeze.

Sycamore

Crusty pale-gray patina flakes from
Smooth irregularly-colored beige under-skin,
Unblemished serrated leaves
Outstretch as open hands, to
Outfit burly arms
Bolstered by buttressed boughs.
Weak and vulnerable nests
Hide among sympathetic ligaments,
With a Zacchaeus's view
Cloaked in shade.
Above the obscure silhouette,
Night owls blink, while
Evening hawks soar.
Deeply buried mesh of roots
With interwoven rocks sink
Below anchored organs.
Sentinel seer.

Hope

Beams of amber sunshine
Tinsel my waking windows, to
Illuminate turquoise skies
This delightful morning.

Streamers of sun rays,
Gift wraps from God,
Presents to unfold
Encourage me to hope.

Hope for the world
For peace and love.
Butterflies
and bluebells,

Twitch in evening wind
To be quiet with summer daisies.
Nature's ubiquitous vestments
Goadingly gravid green.

Roots of Violence

We trace roots of violence
And follow them down
Old cracks of
Earth that
Burned in soil.
Rhizomes of ruthless rage
Twist and knot to
Try to get us mired
In growing weeds.
Infiltrated crevices hide
Below the burly
Tree. Bark destined
From within,
Split in pain
From seeds, bursting
Forth, succulence sustained.
Pebbles caught
Within deep roots
Cause
Festered sores,
Entombed as
Fossils, that cry
Out in pain,
Below the surface
Of the tree.

Expectation

White clouds stream above my head,
beyond my touch.
I look up and wonder
about the meaning of life.

What should I look at?
What do I see past clouds,
Out beyond my touch, beyond my leap?

Why do some hope each day
to touch blue skies and know your love,
your presence,

While others despair
in ashen storm clouds
To block the sun of light
Overhead?

Do they not realize
gray storm clouds bring
Fresh spring rain
to nurture our crops
that feed our souls.
We hope.

The Spirit

Worship the Spirit who made
this world of muted watercolors
mixed with Cynthian beams of light
and hallowed water still.

A saintly dove stands in
the tree above, holding the olive
branch, this time without camouflage.
Down the road a mockingbird

sings its soulful cry while
the crow laughs at the dove
holding its branch without leaves.
Colored tulips begin to sprout

as crocus time is gone. Hyacinths bloom
with the melt of spring snow.
Soon it is time for the robins to
arrive and the worms can hide no more.

Curved Path

I follow the curved path through the woods.
Something drew me down this track
Deep into the timber.

Pine trees tower over me.
Long needles,
Fragrant with the pungent pitch
Permeate tranquil air.

Silence interrupted
A covey of quail brandishing head feathers
As they race to delay our path,
Or we theirs.

Small black-capped chickadees
Flit from bough to bough, to
Make haste across calloused branches.

Lighthearted and carefree,
My heart soars to watch
The performance, the fleeting
Cotillion of the chickadees.

Deep within the stand of pines
I escape life's monotony.
A breath of fresh air,
My spirit galvanized,
Energy inhaled.

A short rest next
To the yellow buttercups
Mixed with blue
Wildflowers yawning
In morning sun, soon
Remind me,

It is back on the curved path
That I must travel.
Revisit the reality of the day,

Away from the quiet respite
Of the gentle, curved path.

Design & Typeset Page

This book was designed by Artistic Design Service. It is set in Adobe Garamond type by Artistic Design Service, and manufactured by Whispering Pine Press International, Inc.

Adobe Garamond

Claude Garamond (c. 1480-1561) worked to develop the Old Face font Garamond. This font has had tremendous influence on the evolution of the typeface developments from the time of its creation to the present. Garamond, or Garamont, is related to the alphabet of Claude Garamond (1480-1561) as well as to the work of Jean Jannon (1580-1635 or 1658), much of which was attributed to Garamond. In comparison to the earlier Italian font forms, Garamond has finer serif and a generally more elegant image. The Garamond of Jean Jannon was introduced at the Paris World's Fair in 1900 as 'Original Garamond', after which many font foundries began to cast similar types. This new interpretation of Garamond, designed by Robert Slimbach, is based on the Original Garamond as a typical Old Face style. However, this font has been expanded to include small caps, expert fonts, and calligraphic caps which were typical of the 15th and 16th centuries.

'Adobe Garamond' is a Trademark of Adobe Systems Incorporated which may be registered in certain jurisdictions.

Index of Poetry

Index by First Line

Reader Feedback Form

Dear Reader,

We are very interested in what our readers think. Please fill in the form below and return it to:

Whispering Pine Press International, Inc.
c/o Frost of Spring Green
Frost of Spring Green Poetry Series – Book 1
P.O. Box 214
Spokane Valley, WA 99037-0214 USA
Phone: (509) 928-8700 | Fax: (509) 922-9949
Email: sales@whisperingpinepress.com
Websites: www.WhisperingPinePress.com
www.WhisperingPinePressBookstore.com
Blog: www.WhisperingPinePressBlog.com

Name: _____

Address: _____

City, St., Zip: _____

Phone/Fax: (___) _____ | (___) _____

Email: _____

Comments/Suggestions: _____

_____

_____

_____

_____

A great deal of care and attention has been exercised in the creation of this book. Although we strive to make this book completely error free, errors and discrepancies may not be completely excluded. If you come across any errors or discrepancies, please make a note of them and send them to our publishing office. We are constantly updating our manuscripts, eliminating errors, and improving quality.

Please contact us at the address above.

We Invite You to Join the
Whispering Pine Press International, Inc.,
Book Club!
Whispering Pine Press International, Inc.

c/o Frost of Spring Green
Frost of Spring Green Poetry Series – Book 1
P.O. Box 214
Spokane Valley, WA 99037-0214 USA
Phone: (509) 928-8700 | Fax: (509) 922-9949
Email: sales@whisperingpinepress.com
Websites: www.WhisperingPinePress.com
www.WhisperingPinePressBookstore.com
Blog: www.WhisperingPinePressBlog.com

Buy 11 books and get the next one free, based on the average price of the first eleven purchased.

How the club works:

Simply use the order form below and order books from our catalog. You can buy just one at a time or all eleven at once. After the first eleven books are purchased, the next one is free. Please add shipping and handling as listed on this form. There are no purchase requirements at any time during your membership. Free book credit is based on the average price of the first eleven books purchased.

Join today! Pick your books and mail in the form today!

Yes! I want to join the Whispering Pine Press International, Inc., Book Club! Enroll me and send the books indicated below.

<u>Title</u>   <u>Price</u>

1._____
2._____
3._____
4._____
5._____
6._____
7._____
8._____
9._____
10._____
11._____

Free Book Title: _____
Free Book Price: _____Avg. Price: _____ Total Price:_ _____
Credit for the free book is based on the average price of the first 11 books purchased.

    (Circle One) Check | Visa | MasterCard | Discover | American Express

Credit Card #: _____Expiration Date:_____
Name:_ _____
Address: _____
City: _____State: _____Country: _____
Zip/Postal: _____ Phone: (_____)_____
Email:_____

    Signature_____

How to Order Autographed Books

To receive a book autographed by the author, Karen Jean Matsko Hood, please fill out the form below completely. Your phone and/or fax numbers are very important for us to have so we can contact you to clarify information if needed.

If you do not want to place your order online or if this page is temporarily not working, please fill out the following form, copy and paste it into an email, or print it and fax or mail it to:

Whispering Pine Press International, Inc.
c/o Frost of Spring Green
Frost of Spring Green Poetry Series – Book 1
P.O. Box 214
Spokane Valley, WA 99037-0214 USA
Phone: (509) 928-8700 | Fax: (509) 922-9949
Email: sales@whisperingpinepress.com
Websites: www.WhisperingPinePress.com
www.WhisperingPinePressBookstore.com
Blog: www.WhisperingPinePressBlog.com

Date: _____

Name: _____

Address:_____

City:_____

State: _____ Zip: _____ Country: _____

Phone: _____ Fax: _____

Email: _____

Autograph Information:

Unless otherwise requested, the author will simply autograph the book(s) requested. If you would like a message along with the author's signature, please describe what you would like her to write.

_____

_____

_____

_____

_____

Whispering Pine Press International, Inc. Order Form

Gift-wrapping, Autographing, and Inscription

We are proud to offer personal autographing by the author. For a limited time this service is absolutely free! Gift-wrapping is also available for $4.95 per item.

1. Sold To

Name: _____
Street/Route: _____
_____
City: _____
State: _____ Zip: _____
Country: _____
Gift message: _____
_____
Email address: _____
Daytime Phone: (_ _ _) _ _ _-_ _ _ _
*Necessary for verifying orders
Home Phone: (_ _ _) _ _ _-_ _ _ _
Fax: (_ _ _) _ _ _-_ _ _ _

2. Ship To

☐ Is this a new or corrected address?

☐ Alternative Shipping Address

☐ Mailing Address

Name: _____
Address: _____
_____
City: _____
State: _____ Zip: _____
Country: _____
Email address: _____

3. Items Ordered

ISBN # /Item #	Size	Color	Qty.	Title or Description	Price	Total

4. Method Of Payment

International, Inc. (No Cash or COD's)

☐ Visa ☐ MasterCard ☐ Discover ☐ American Express ☐ Check/Money Order

Please make it payable to Whispering Pine Press International, Inc. (No Cash or COD's)

Account Number   Expiration Date
                              _____ / _____
                              Month   Year

☐☐☐☐ ☐☐☐☐ ☐☐☐☐ ☐☐☐☐

Signature_____
                Cardholder's signature
Printed Name_____
           Please print name of cardholder
Address of Cardholder_____

Subtotal	
Gift wrap $4.95 Each	
For delivery in WA add 8.7% sales tax.	
Shipping See chart at left	
6. Total	

5. Shipping & Handling

Continental US

US Postal Ground: For books please add $4.95 for the first book and $2.95 each for additional books.
All non-book items, add 15% of the Subtotal.
Please allow 1-4 weeks for delivery.
US Postal Air: Please add $15.00 shipping and handling.
Please allow 1-3 days for delivery.
Alaska, Hawaii, and the US Territories By Ship:
Please add 10% shipping and handling (minimum charge $15.00).

Please
By Air: Please add 12% shipping and handling (minimum charge $15.00).
Please allow 2–6 weeks for delivery.
International By Ship: Please add 10% shipping and handling (minimum charge $15.00).
Please allow 6-12 weeks for delivery.
By Air: Please add 12% shipping and handling (minimum charge $15.00).
Please allow 2-6 weeks for delivery.
FedEx Shipments: Add $5.00 to the above airmail charges for overnight delivery.

Shop Online:
www.whisperingpinepress.com
Fax orders to: (509) 922-9949

Whispering Pine Press International, Inc.
P.O. Box 214
Spokane Valley, WA 99037-0214 USA
Phone: (509) 928-8700 • Fax: (509) 922-9949
Email: sales@whisperingpinepress.com
Website: www.whisperingpinepress.com

About the Poet

Karen Jean Matsko Hood began writing as a shy author, but has now developed a voice that is all her own. Hood exhibits a unique story as well as a voice of empathy and purpose. Hood's writing is strong-minded. She is a meticulous wordsmith and combines stories with compassion. Hood has always loved children and is devoted to the needs of children. It is only natural that she would channel her efforts to include children's books and poetry.

Hood reminds us of the importance of our links with nature and environment in our daily lives. Her writing carries the urgency and outrage of the current social injustice and inequality. The recurring theme in Hood's work is to provide a voice for those whose struggle cannot be heard. Hood's writing brings poignancy to the most hopeless of situations. She is romantic in her vision for a quest for dignity and social justice.

Hood also writes about personal and spiritual themes. She is passionate both as a feminist and as an active children's rights advocate. Hood also works to encourage literacy for all ages. Her blend of traditionalism and modernism brings a current freshness and uniqueness to her own poetic voice. She is versatile in her writing style and is able to incorporate a wide range of themes and topics. Her poems have been published in a myriad of magazines and publications.

Hood was born and raised in Great Falls, Montana. As an undergraduate, she attended the College of St. Benedict in St. Joseph, Minnesota, and St. John's University in Collegeville, Minnesota. She attended the University of Great Falls in Great Falls, Montana. Hood received a B.S. Degree in Natural Science from the College of St. Benedict and minored in both Psychology and Secondary Education. Upon her graduation, Hood and her husband taught science and math on the island of St. Croix in the U.S. Virgin Islands. Hood has completed postgraduate classes at the University of Iowa in Iowa City, Iowa. In May 2001, she completed her Master's Degree in Pastoral Ministry at Gonzaga University in Spokane, Washington. She has taken postgraduate classes at Lewis and Clark College on the North Idaho college campus in Coeur d'Alene, Idaho, and Taylor University in Fort Wayne, Indiana. Hood is working on research projects to complete her Ph.D. in Leadership Studies at Gonzaga University in Spokane, Washington.

Hood resides in Greenacres, Washington, along with her husband, many of her seventeen children, and foster children. Her interests include writing, research, and teaching. She previously has volunteered as a court advocate in the Spokane juvenile court system for abused and neglected children. Hood is a literary advocate for youth and adults. Her hobbies include cooking, baking, collecting, photography, indoor and outdoor gardening, farming, and the cultivation of unusual flowering plants and orchids. She enjoys raising several specialty breeds of animals including

Babydoll Southdown, Friesen, and Icelandic sheep, Icelandic horses, bichons frisés, cockapoos, Icelandic sheepdogs, a Newfoundland, a Rottweiler, a variety of Nubian and fainting goats, and a few rescue cats. Hood also enjoys bird-watching and finds all aspects of nature precious.

She demonstrates a passionate appreciation of the environment and a respect for all life. She also invites you to visit her websites:

www.KarenJeanMatskoHood.com
www.KarenJeanMatskoHoodBookstore.com
www.KarenJeanMatskoHoodBlog.com
www.KarensKidsBooks.com
www.KarensTeenBooks.com

www.HoodFamilyBlog.com
www.HoodFamily.com

Author's Social Media
Like or Friend the Author on Facebook:
https://www.facebook.com/KarenJeanMatskoHoodAuthorFanPage
Follow the Author on Twitter: https://twitter.com/KarenJeanHood
Google Plus Profile: http://google.com/+KarenJeanMatskoHood
Pinterest: https://www.pinterest.com/KarenJMHood/
LinkedIn: http://www.linkedin.com/in/KarenJeanMatskoHood
YouTube: http://www.youtube.com/KarenJeanMatskoHood
Instagram: http://instagram.com/KarenJeanMatskoHood
MySpace: https://myspace.com/KarenJeanMatskoHood

www.ingramcontent.com/pod-product-compliance
Lightning Source LLC
Chambersburg PA
CBHW031248090426
42742CB00007B/368